Beach Cottages

Beach Cottages

Publisher: **Paco Asensio**

Editor: **Haike Falkenberg**

Editorial coordination: **Alejandro Bahamón**

Translation: **Juliet King**

Documentation: **Marta Casado Lorenzo**

Art director: **Mireia Casanovas Soley**

Layout: **Gisela Legares Gili**

2002 © Loft Publications S.L. and HBI,
an imprint of HarperCollins International

First published in 2002 by LOFT and HBI,
an imprint of HarperCollins International
10 East 53rd St., New York, NY 10022-5299

Distributed in the U.S. and Canada by Watson-Guptill Publications
770 Broadway, New York, NY 10003-9595
Telephone: (800) 451-1741 or (732) 363-4511 in NJ, AK, HI Fax: (732) 363-0338

ISBN: 0-8230-0478-3

Distributed throughout the rest of the world by
HarperCollins International
10 East 53rd St. New York, NY 10022-5299
Fax: (212) 207-7654

ISBN: 0-06-008684-X
D.L.: B-13.250-2002

Editorial project:
LOFT Publications
Domènech, 9 2-2
08012 Barcelona. Spain
Tel.: +34 93 218 30 99
Fax.: +34 93 237 00 60
e-mail:loft@loftpublications.com
www.loftpublications.com

If you would like to suggest projects for inclusion in our next volumes, please e-mail details to us at:
loft@loftpublications.com

Printed in: Viking.Barcelona, Spain

March 2002

danielson house — 10
Brian MacKay-Lyons

tagomago house — 18
Carlos Ferrater + Joan Guibernau

house in cavalli beach — 26
Chris Howe Architect

reyna residence — 32
Dean Nota Architect

b house — 38
Barclay – Crousse Architects

m house — 46
Barclay – Crousse Architects

house in bay of islands — 52
Pete Bossley Architect

the rock of las hadas island — 58
Alberto Burckhardt

light house — 66
Lehrer Architects

medlands beach house — 72
Arquitectus

berk rauch residence — 78
Stelle Architects

winer residence — 84
Stelle Architects

house in barnegat light — 92
Brian Healy & Michael Ryan

yallingup residence — 96
Considine and Griffiths Architects Pty. Ltd.

house in formentera — 102
Bill Wright + Nacho Alonso

cohen house — 108
Toshiko Mori Architect

house lødner egge — 116
div.A arkitekter

ocean house — 120
Cox Richardson

summer cabin — 126
Jarmund / Vigsnaes AS Architects MNAL

carmen house — 132
Leddy Maytum Stacy Architects

vally martelli house — 142
Mario Connío

koehler residence — 148
Julie Snow Architects

merimbula house — 156
Clinton Murray Architects Pty. Ltd.

coromandel house — 164
Fearon Hay Architects

house in long beach island — 170
Brian Healy & Michael Ryan

directory — 176

1

2

3

Building a beach cottage is one of the most appetizing projects for both architects and for people who love the seashore. The beach landscape has special characteristics. As the boundary between the land and the sea, the terrain is subject to extreme conditions with great climatic variability. **1** The intensity of the sun or wind can change drastically in only a few hours. At the same time, the large mass of water works as a thermostat to absorb the heat during the day and to give it off at night, producing minimal fluctuations in temperature. The building sites enjoy marvelous views whose composition is dominated by the horizon and by various shades of blue. The vegetation, punished by the extreme climate, features formal characteristics. **2** The flora might include tall, svelte palm trees that frame the visual or large, tree-like masses ranging from dense forests to small shrubs that are placed like a cover above the topography. Finally, the terrain makes it difficult to lay the foundations for any construction. The rocky geography creates complicated situations and the presence of sand causes continuous changes in the level of the ground.**3**

The fascinating and natural conditions of the coast, which are difficult to tackle, are the framework for these twenty-five projects scattered around the world. The owners use the cottages as second homes. Therefore, their use –which is different from a conventional residence– determines the important factors for each project. These houses are designed to accommodate occupants for short periods of time throughout the year, to house two or more family groups, or to serve as cabins that fulfill the basic needs for living.**4** Yet, this is not the reason why the projects are reduced to basic proposals or elementary architectural language. On the contrary, each cottage presents a design of great creativity and sophistication, even though it may seem simple at first glance. The possible solutions span as wide a range as the project's geographical locations. For example, the projects of Barclay and Crousse on the coasts of Peru present forceful volumes that create a wide range of full and empty planes, **5** while Brian Healy and Michael Ryan's proposals in New Jersey, **6** in the United States achieve a fine filigree of textures in the surfaces. Both architectural teams tackle the same theme with formal results that are different, yet appropriate for the house's environment.

4

5

A refined analysis of these determinants, natural or requested by the client, are reflected in the way that the building is placed in the landscape and how the fine details and finishes are resolved. Following this same process of analysis, each one of the projects is understood through these common patterns on which all are based to achieve the desired result. First, is the position: how the building is placed with respect to the movement of the sun, the breezes, the views or the neighboring constructions. Careful observation guarantees the correct thermal conditioning of a house by taking advantage of the sun in the winter and in the summer. The Koheler residence by Julie Snow Architects **7** not only makes the most of the sunlight by organizing the house along the east-west axis; it places the building only a few yards from the line of the high tide, the highest in the world, at the Bay of Fundy, Canada.

6

Bay of Fundy

7

8

9

10

The volumetric, dimensions and relationships between the structures that form the projects are generally short in height when the proportions of the site permit it. What dominates is a fragmented composition that creates a multitude of volumes and exterior spaces, achieving a better relationship with the exterior but also helping to make the different areas of the project independent. In works like Casa Carmen by Leddy Maytum Stacy Architects, **8** elements like terraces, patios, long paths and balconies are basic parts of the composition. In more urban surroundings and sites with narrow proportions, the scheme is reduced to only a single, compact volume that incorporates an interior opening in the form of a courtyard. The height of the building is elevated, producing vertical relationships and large openings towards only one side of the house. This is the case with the projects by Lehrer Architects and Dan Nota on the crowded beaches of California.**9**

The formal language and the configuration of a project's exterior and interior elements come from a basic scheme. In every case, the architectural plan tries to emphasize the fundamental concepts of the composition, focusing the house towards a large opening or isolating it by using minimal gestures and materials, like continual planes with few windows. The frames of the doors and windows have a minimal sections and, in many cases, the glass is built into the walls, emphasizing the relationship with the impressive visual. The structural system, which in all cases is basic, is generally exposed and forms an integral part of the architecture and the interior decoration. The structure is noticeably visible in the cottages built by Chris Howe **10** and Pete Bossley in New.Zealand.**11**

11

12

13

Finally, the materials, a fundamental part of each project, end up consolidating the light character of each house while striking up a dialogue with the traditions of the place. Noble materials, like wood, stone and metal, are used to represent the architectural style of each region, yet are reinterpreted in a contemporary language. As a result, we find different textures like the white stone surfaces of Casa Togomago by Carlos Ferrater **12**, which uses the natural stone of the island of Ibiza, in Spain. Alberto Burckhardt´s project on the Islas del Rosario, in Colombia, features artisanal work in macana, a typical wood from the Caribbean region.**13**

Beach Cottages is a compilation that condenses and illustrates different ways of approaching a particular type of residence, half way between the modern house and the vernacular home. The fundamental premise is the relationship with the environment and the desire to create an extremely relaxing atmosphere.

The Danielson house is a small refuge, designed as a place to stay for short periods of time. Despite a limited budget, the architects managed to create a sober and elegant architectural structure. Two factors greatly influenced the project's design: the professions of the clients, a meteorologist and a landscape architect, and the impressive location of the site.

The residence is surrounded by the typical forest found on the coast of Nova Scotia, in the extreme east of Canada. The lot sits at the edge of a small cliff. The elevation of the land with respect to the beach makes it possible to enjoy panoramic views of Aspy Bay and the North Cape. The composition is organized along a longitudinal wooden platform that is parallel to the line of the sea. Two separate buildings house the different functions of the residence. The small one, attached to the wooden platform, contains storage, while the larger one, placed above the platform, contains the rest of the functions.

The interior scheme features the same simplicity as the general floor plan. The service and storage areas are grouped –following the longitudinal sense of the space– in the back part, which looks onto the forest. The back façade is mostly closed. The living room is located on the other side and serves as an extension of the wooden platform inside. From here, the residents can appreciate a view of the sea thanks to the completely transparent façade. Two narrow wooden staircases lead to a loft above the service zone, which contains the sleeping quarters.

In order to keep costs down and take full advantage of the short construction period due to the seasons, the project was mostly prefabricated in Halifax. The technique of building a structure and then assembling it on the site comes from the legacy of boat construction, a traditional industry of the area. Thanks to this solution, the house was built quickly and within the budget. The refuge was also treated to endure the extreme climatic conditions of the zone.

Architect: **Brian MacKay-Lyons Architecture**

Collaborators: **Bruno Weber, Trevor Davies, Darryl Jonas**

Location: **Smelt Brook, Nova Scotia, Canada**

Surface area: **2,677 square feet**

Date: **1998**

Photographer: **Undine Pröhl**

danielʃon houʃe

Brian MacKay-Lyons

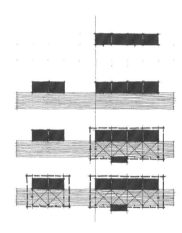

This refined project has great spatial quality due to the clever contrast of three elements: a wooden platform and two light volumes.

The isolation of the house, in the middle of a pine forest and at the high part of a cliff, made it impossible to closely link the interior and the exterior. The longitudinal wooden terrace is the principal element of the cabin's composition.

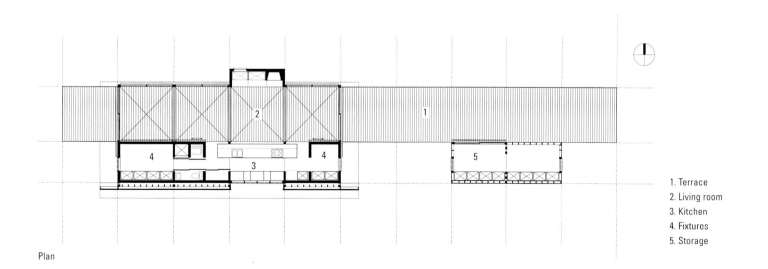

1. Terrace
2. Living room
3. Kitchen
4. Fixtures
5. Storage

Plan

The zinc roof, which wraps around the structure as if it were a folded paper, is exposed, making reference to the cabin's industrial character. Most of the pieces used to build the cabin were prefabricated in Halifax.

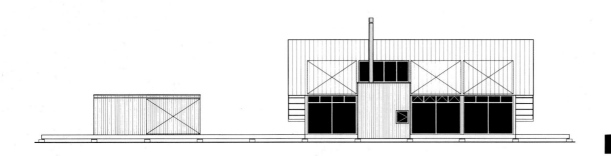

Elevation

Transversal section

A composition of wooden panels creates a solid element that breaks the transparency of the north façade. This area includes a chimney, some closets and a built-in sofa that complements the living room furnishings and enjoys the view through a small window.

This house overlooks the sea on the island of Tagomago in Ibiza, Spain. The landscape is typically Mediterranean, with pine trees and ravines. The land has a light slope that ends in a steep cliff, like a balcony with vistas towards a flat horizon. The intense light, the green forest and the blue sea frame this property of austere and still forms.

A family vacation home, the residence is organized around a principal nucleus and a series of small structures or pavilions that enjoy a certain autonomy. This layout gives the project flexibility according to the number of people that are there at any given time. The building is organized across a longitudinal axis that links all the rooms with the nucleus, offering isolated and independent areas that enjoy an optimal orientation. In addition, the composition of distinct, isolated volumes created a series of open spaces that form patios, porches and terraces. These spaces blur the limits between the interior and the exterior. The longitudinal axis finishes off the guest room, which features a terrace solarium above it.

The living room opens onto a large wooden terrace overlooking the pool, flanked by a large canopy of reinforced concrete. The rooms that make up the nucleus of the house include a hallway, living room, dining room, kitchen, services and master bedroom with bath. A patio separates the central volume from the four small pavilions for the children, which could easily be renovated should the family grow in the future.

The architects used traditional materials for the construction that are typical of the region, such as stone for the façades and walls and wood for the carpentry and terrace floors. The partitions are traditional and are made out of concrete beams and small ceramic vaults. In the solid volumes, the wall above the window prevails. In the living room, a large continuous window protects it from the sun with an eave that crosses its entire length to offer a wide view of the surroundings and to communicate the interior with the terrace and the pool.

tagomago House

Carlos Ferrater + Joan Guibernau

The rectilinear forms that make up this complex of simple, austere volumes emphasize the materials: the white stone and concrete contrast with the dark wood of the terrace.

Architects: **Carlos Ferrater and Joan Guibernau**
Location: **San Carlos, Ibiza, Spain**
Surface area: **8,065 square feet**
Date: **2001**
Photographer: **Alejo Bagué**

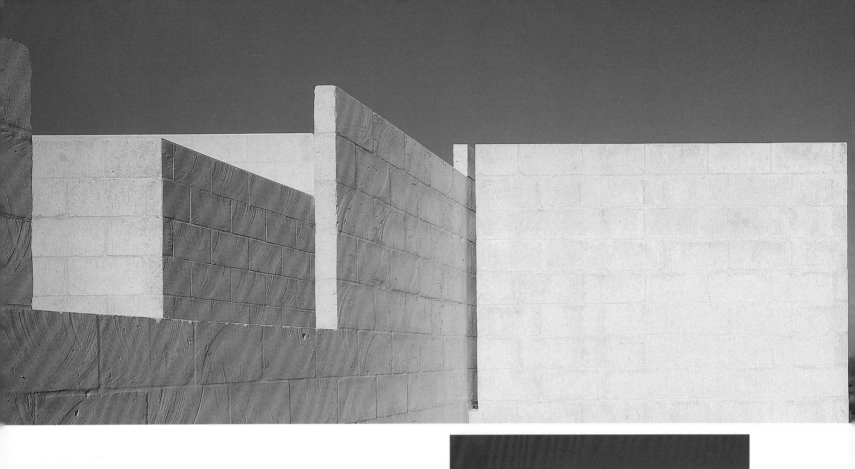

1. Entrance
2. Living room
3. Dining room
4. Kitchen
5. Main bedroom
6. Terrace
7. Swimming pool
8. Bedrooms
9. Guest room

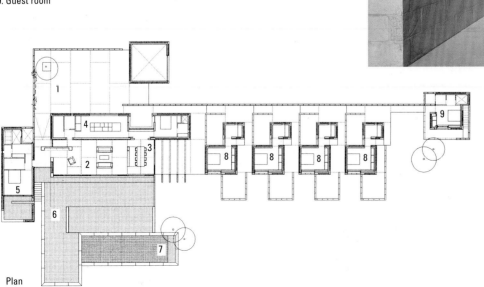

Plan

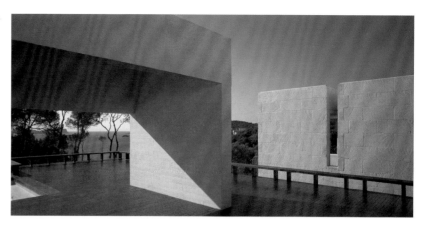

The pool, situated in front of the living room, is surrounded by a wooden platform that overlooks the surrounding view. A large portico is placed between the two spaces, creating a covered exterior zone that also filters the light that shines inside.

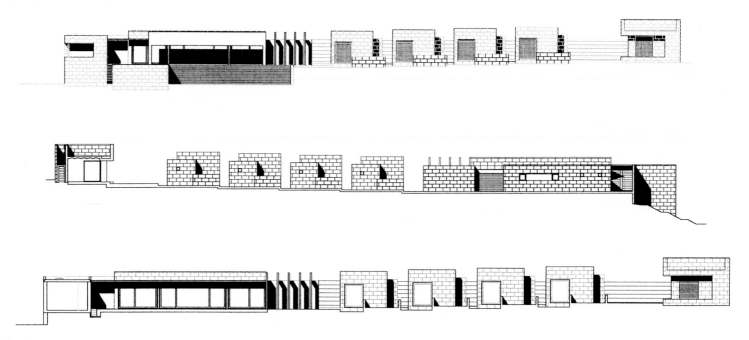

Sections

The architectural language of the house, even though it has a solid and contemporary character, respects the island's traditional architecture by using local materials, including stone and wood.

The layout of the walls generates openings towards the exterior. Large windows framed in natural-colored wood stretch from one extreme to the other.

The furnishings selected for the interior reflect the sober and forceful lines of the house's architecture. The continuity of the space is emphasized by the low sofas and the opening of the furniture that divides the dining room from the living room.

The owners of this house and guest pavilion, located on a remote bay in the north of New Zealand, asked the architect to design a project that would have the minimum possible impact on the environment. They requested that the construction use local materials and had a limited budget. The architect's objective, therefore, was to create a home that would meet these requirements and that would balance comfort, design and vernacular references. The architectural concept is based on the principle that the building must be in contact with the ground and that it must respect the majestic landscape. The result is an object in the form of a shell that hugs the curve of the hill. The building is related to both the hill and the sea.

The construction, located on an old geological fault, is supported by 60 wooden pillars that recall the extensive Kauri forest that covered this region before the arrival of the European colonies in the nineteenth century. The owners reforested the terrain surrounding the house with native trees and exotic palms, which make reference to the area's Polynesian origins. The three levels that make up the building are placed under the curved plane of the continuous roof, which was constructed using wooden, laminated beams that the repeat the form of the hill. On the lower level, there are three bedrooms and bathrooms for guests, which open onto the wooden terrace toward the north, capturing the dramatic view of the bay. The middle level contains a large open space used as a living area and a dining room, adjacent to the kitchen, garage and entrance. A sliding glass window runs along the entire living area and dining room, linking the interior with another wooden terrace that leans towards the north and makes a cut in the roof. The upper level, which is reached from the living room, contains the master bedroom, bathroom and a small private study.

The architect carefully selected the interior and exterior details and materials in order to keep costs down and to create a dialogue with the history of the setting. Inside, the pillars are tied with linen fabrics produced by the Maori, who also made the rugs. The wood used inside the house and for the structure is radiated pine, a popular variety of the region.

Houſe in cavalli beach

Chris Howe Architect

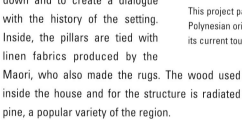

This project pays homage to the rich diversity of the area, including its Polynesian origins, the first European settlers, the local Maori culture and its current touristic image.

Architect: **Chris Howe**

Collaborators: **Martyn Evans Architects**

Location: **Rapaki Beach, Northland, New Zealand**

Surface area: **4,700 square feet**

Date: **1998**

Photographers: **Patrick Reynolds and Chris Howe**

A continual roof, supported on both extremes of the terrain, is the most important element of the project's composition. The openings towards the exterior terraces enjoy views of the bay and reveal their wooden structure.

Ground floor

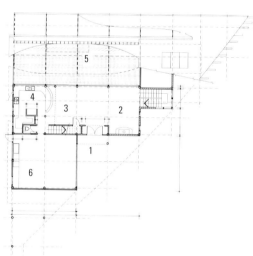

First floor

1. Entrance
2. Living room
3. Dining room
4. Kitchen
5. Terrace
6. Parking
7. Main Bedroom
8. Studio
9. Bedrooms
10. Children´s studio

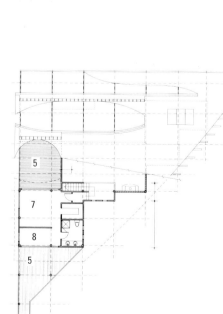

Second floor

The sliding doors that compose the back façade leave the interior space free, connecting it directly with the longitudinal terrace that crosses the house. The wood furnishings complement the exposed structure and the exterior details, made of the same material.

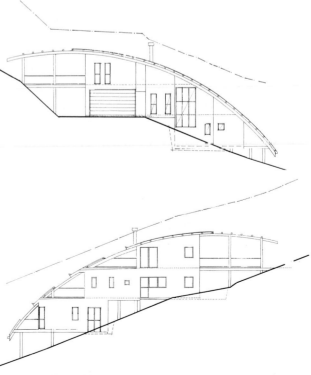

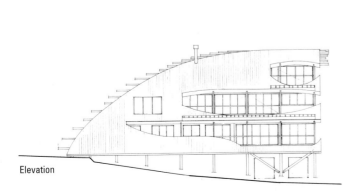

Elevation

This house is located on a 30 x 79-foot lot situated on the marine front of Hermosa Beach, a coastal settlement in the western part of the Los Angeles metropolitan area. The lot's longitudinal axis is demarcated on the northern and southern sides by adjacent residences. A pedestrian walkway, known as The Strand, borders the beach on the west side and vehicle access is provided from the east. The setting's dominant physical characteristic is the views of the beach and the ocean framed by a pier in the north, and of the Palos Verdes Peninsula and Santa Catalina Island in the south. Hermosa Beach is an environment in transition, which mixes small, older structures with contemporary architectural structures of a bigger scale.

The client required a residence for one or two people and occasional guests. The idea was to provide access to the public life and social interaction of the pedestrian walkway, while creating a more private ambience for entertainment and rest. The layout is thus organized in a vertical sequence of three levels, which ascend toward the most private space. A guest room, family room and parking are located on the ground floor next to the double entrance. The living room, dining room, kitchen and a second bedroom occupy the two intermediate levels, while the master bedroom and bathroom are located on the top floor to take advantage of the best views.

The circulation begins with the double entrance, which connects on one side to the pedestrian walkway and to the street and parking on the other. This modest and austere entrance leads to a spatial experience that expands in a sequence articulated by the stairway, which connects the different areas of house. The arrival at each level reveals a space that opens progressively to the light and the ocean views. Each one of the three floors extends to the exterior with terraces that overlook the oceanfront.

reYNd reſideNce

33

Dean Nota Architect

The heart of the house is a large space that contains the living areas and is directly related to the beach by way of a large glass surface.

Architect: **Dean Nota Architect AIA**
Collaborators: **Stephen Billings, Josep Fedorowich, Marina Mizruh (interior design)**
Location: **Hermosa Beach, California, United States**
Surface area: **3,440 square feet**
Date: **2000**
Photographer: **Erhard Pfeiffer**

On the eastern façade, the house is presented as a closed and solid volume. On the front facing the beach, it appears as a completely transparent object open to the sea. The house's solid materials contrast with the lightness of the roof and the inclined form of the back façade.

Second floor

First floor

1. Entrance
2. Parking
3. Living room
4. Bedrooms
5. Terrace
6. Living room
7. Dining room
8. Kitchen
9. Main bedroom
10. Terrace

Ground floor

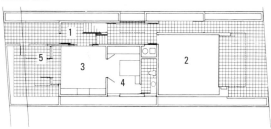

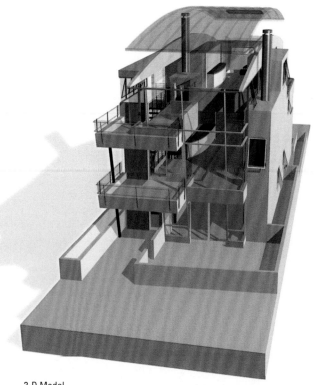

3-D Model

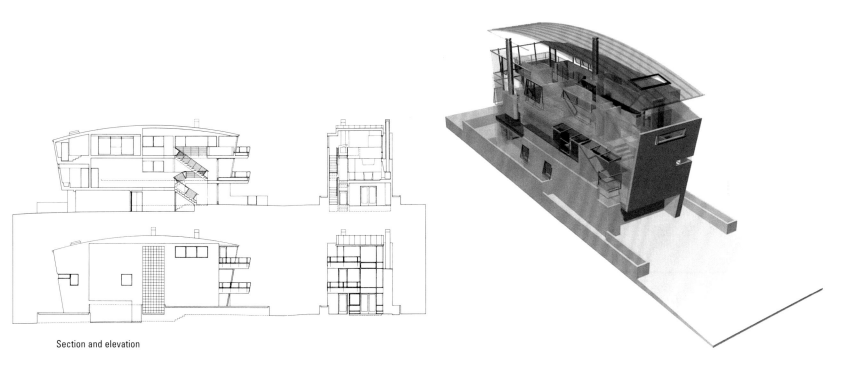

Section and elevation

The balconies, enormous pieces that lean towards the ocean, seem to float in the middle of the large glass façade on the back part of the house. The juxtaposition of exterior spaces, the interior walkway and the large window endow the interior with spatial richness.

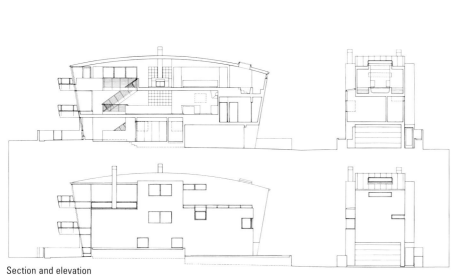

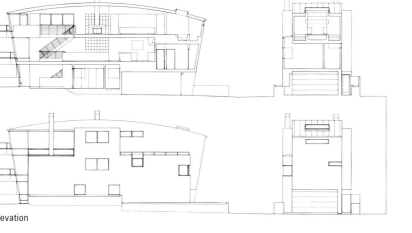

Section and elevation

This project began with an analysis of the environment surrounding the site. Even though the land is located in one of the most arid deserts of the world, its climatic conditions are not extreme, since temperatures vary between 59°F in winter and 84°F in summer. There is also an imperceptible temperature variation between the day and the night. The challenge was to create a totally permeable architecture in which the walls emphasize the landscape and provide just enough privacy to make the building habitable. Architectural abstraction linked the work to architectural and artistic expressions from the region's pre-Columbian and Spanish colonial periods.

Building the house on such a steep hillside made it possible to open only one façade to the exterior. The next obligatory step was to separate the walls in order to create different ways of relating them to the sea landscape and to make the most of the only view. Finally, the architecture had to meet the requirements of a family that required separate spaces for the parents and children, leading to a generational separation in the vertical sense. The house is divided into three levels, united by an exterior stairway. A social area separates the parent's level on the upper floor from the children's quarters on the lower level.

The staircase is the axis that structures the project, as well as the element that unites the distinct levels of the house with one another and the beach. Since the staircase is located on the exterior, it gives each level functional autonomy. Its configuration reveals the slope of the land and frames the view towards the sea. The house is entered from the top of the hill, at the roof, where a platform also serves as a parking area.

Each level has a specific complementary activity that relates to a vertical wall that connects it in a distinct manner with the landscape. The social level features a large terrace, designed as a summer salon and partially protected by a pergola that detaches from the wall. A horizontal fissure frames the sea and a neighboring island.

The parents´ level has a more intimate exterior zone, treated as a solarium supported by the wall and forming a balcony towards the view. Finally, the children's level includes a television room in which the wall serves as blinds that diffuse the intensity of the light and frame the visual across a vertical gap.

b Houſe

Barclay-Crousse Architects

This project arose from a reflection on three essential factors: the climatic conditions of the Peruvian coast, the geographic conditions of the site and the special needs of the client.

Architect: **Sandra Barclay and Jean Pierre Crousse**

Collaborators: **Carlos Casabone (structure)**

Location: **The Escondida beach, Cañete, Peru**

Surface: **2,839 square feet**

Date: **1999**

Photographer: **Roberto Huarcaya**

This house's spectacular geographic location was a challenge for the architects who strove to make the most of the surrounding landscape. The building is embedded in half of the slope, emphasizing the project's direction towards the ocean view.

Location plan

As an object that hangs down from the high part of the slope, the building is vertical, with multiple spatial relationships between the different levels and the sea. A series of terraces, solariums and exterior zones develop towards the beach.

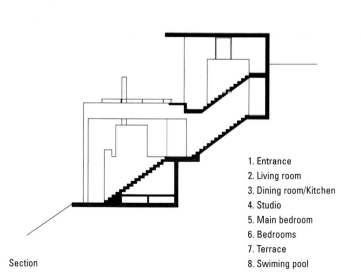

Section

1. Entrance
2. Living room
3. Dining room/Kitchen
4. Studio
5. Main bedroom
6. Bedrooms
7. Terrace
8. Swiming pool

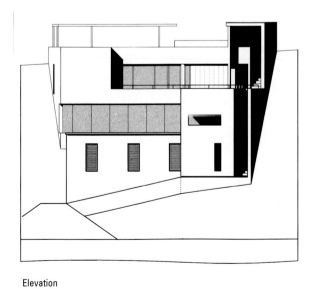

Elevation

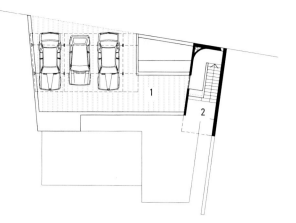

Third floor

Second floor

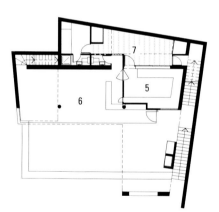

First floor

Ground floor

1. Parking
2. Entrance
3. Main room
4. Guest room
5. Kitchen
6. Dining room
7. Terrace
8. Living
9. Bedrooms

The clarity and force of the scheme created clear and luminous spaces that frame the view from different perspectives. While strong colors are used on the exterior to contrast with the monochromatic landscape, the interior features a range of whites that create a fresh, relaxed atmosphere.

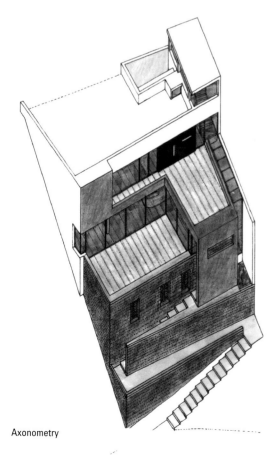

Axonometry

This project's composition posed a challenge: to resolve and value the dual conditions of the site. As a house in the desert, the building had to create an intimate space amidst the vast landscape. On the other hand, the presence of the ocean called for the house to open up towards the horizon. The architectural plans started with this contradiction: to establish a dialectical relationship between closure and opening, opacity and transparency, intimacy and exteriority, and tradition and modernity.

The house's composition reintroduces characteristics of traditional construction on the Peruvian coast. The simple, closed volumes form a composition of masses that integrate with the abstract desert landscape. Following local building traditions, the architects first established a site and then demarcated the land with walls that preserve the intimacy of the exterior zones, while relating them to the interior space of the house.

The house is divided into three areas that contain its different functions. The first consists of parking and the entrance. The children's bedrooms and the guest quarters occupy the central volume, while the parent's bedroom – situated above the living room, dining room and kitchen – makes up the third. The real dimensions of the site are visible from the living room, the principal area of the house, and give it a sensation of great amplitude. The circulations are installed between the volumes like cracks formed on land dried up by the sun.

The areas create relationships among one another, producing imbalances of the land that permit the residents to perceive the ocean from even the most remote spots. The limits between the interior and exterior fade due to the use of light and transparency and glass without frames, and to the treatment of the materials. The sequence first leads to an elongated patio that follows the slope of the land with a soft staircase. The sea and the nearby island, found in the axis of this space, are framed by a large, double-height horizontal opening that makes up the living area. The path then leads to a terrace, where there is a pool, in the form of the balcony, above the cliff and the sea.

M Houſe

Barclay-Crousse Architects

This project resulted from a meditation on the dichotomy of building on the Peruvian coast, which mixes two distinct landscapes: the arid desert and a view of the sea.

Architect: **Sandra Barclay and Jean Pierre Crousse**

Collaborators: **Carlos Casabone (structure)**

Location: **The Escondida beach, Cañete, Peru**

Surface: **1,785 square feet**

Date: **2001**

Photographer: **Jean Pierre Crousse**

The northwest façade, which will include another construction in the near future, is a composition of planes and solid volumes. The southern façade is a large, transparent opening that enjoys views of the sea.

Location plan

1. Parking
2. Entrance
3. Bedrooms
4. Main room
5. Living room/Dining room
6. Kitchen
7. Terrace
8. Swimming pool

First floor

Ground floor

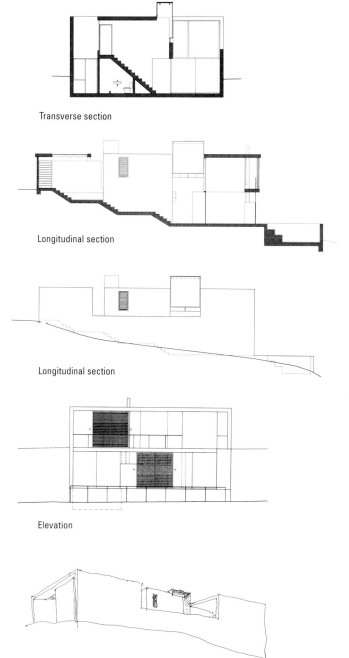

Transverse section

Longitudinal section

49

Longitudinal section

Elevation

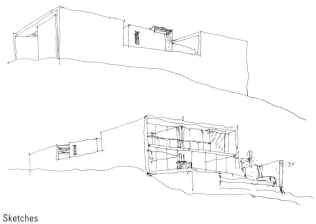

Sketches

The project's play of volumes creates various scenarios in which the sea is ever-present and framed by architectural elements like porticos and large windows. The chromatic play complements this diversity and contrasts with the surroundings.

In contrast to the solid materials with which the house is built, elements like glass, wooden platforms and blinds offer a counterpoint of lightness, linking the project to the regional architecture.

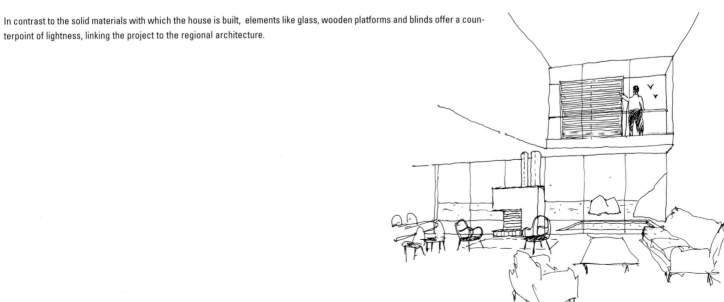

This vacation house is a family refuge set in a location of great natural beauty, in the Bay of Islands, in the northern part of New Zealand. A sanctuary to escape the overcrowded world, the house has a close relationship with the exterior. In honor of the setting, the building emphasizes and enriches the island experience.

The project is basically a large composition of elements that were constructed on the mainland and assembled on the island. The house meets the requirements of an isolated home with elements of twentieth century architecture. The search for a precise and structurally expressive architectural language inspired the architect to create the home out of wood, the material par excellence in New Zealand. Bossley also explored the influence of the Group Architects, who became national legends in the mid-twentieth century. Due to the home's transparency and three-dimensional spatial fluidity, it recalls the Maison Carre by Alvar Aalto.

Many settlements in New Zealand are located in transitional zones along the coasts. Most houses built on the bays tend to follow the colonial tradition which placed the building in the center of the lot. This residence differs in that it is located on the side of the land, under some existing trees. The architect combined the idea of sleeping in the open air with a shed for boats to create a camp-like structure, with

Architect: **Pete Bossley**
Collaborators: **James Downey, Andrea Bell, Don McKenzie**
Location: **Bay of Islands, New Zealand**
Surface: **3,763 square feet**
Date: **1997**
Photographer: **Patrick Reynolds**

House in bay of islands

Pete Bossley Architect

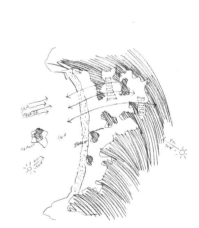

an appropriate scale, that lives in its surroundings rather than dominates them. The luminosity of the house as well as the structure that sustains a large roof create a certain sense of temporariness, appropriate to a vacation home. From the exterior, the house looks more like a shop than a residence.

The construction used wooden applications that required great precision from fine artisans. The exterior walls feature carpentry from top to bottom, while the interior walls are covered with cedar panels to the height of the doors and then with glass to the ceiling. The 132-foot-long roof floats above the walls and is supported by a structure of slender wooden frames.

This cabin embodies the process of construction and composition and the balance between structure and form, creating a sense of intimacy, richness and presence in the interior space.

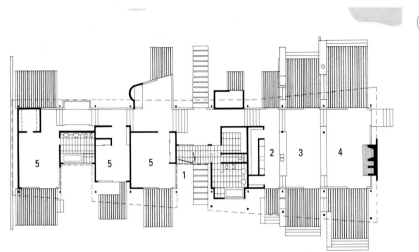

1. Entrance
2. Kitchen
3. Dining room
4. Living room
5. Bedrooms

54 Plan

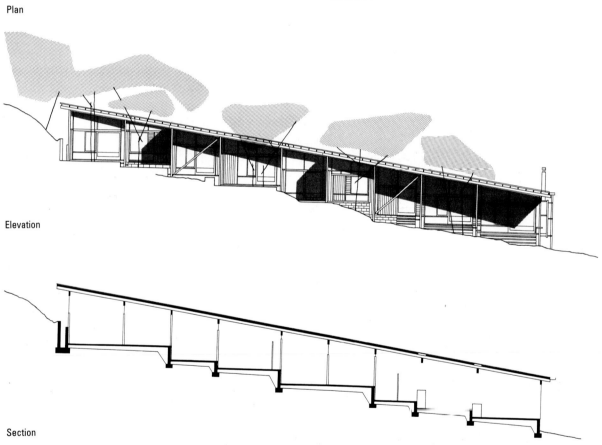

Elevation

Section

Due to the difficulty of constructing on the island, the house is made mostly of prefabricated elements that were assembled on the site. The structure is made entirely of wooden frames.

The linear layout follows a north-south axis, staggering the land on eight different levels clearly defined by structural wood frames that the walls leave free. The house's width is adjusted according to the needs of the rooms, which all have a view of the beach.

This project is located on a small island, composed of two small cays that form part of the Archipelago Natural Park on the Rosario Islands, in Colombia. After years of abandonment, the island was in an advanced state of deterioration. The planning process started with a global concept of the land. The architect consolidated the existing elements and incorporated new architectural elements to create a recreational residence. The project included the reforestation of the small island and the construction of two access piers and protective walls on the perimeter. The architect also took advantage of the remains of an old house and a small kiosk.

The project's main challenge was to transform the existing house, a composition with modern lines, into a building appropriate for the Caribbean atmosphere. Even though the architect respected the original placement of the house, he demolished a large part of it, leaving only the basic structure. The new residence developed from there, and the architect carefully studied the openings to give the interior spaces a 360-degree view of the site. To insure a cool atmosphere inside the house, a study of the breezes and the sun determined the composition.

The use of artisan elements created an architectural language appropriate for the place without hiding the house's modern origins. Special features of the project include the pergolas that filter the light, the rattan rails with ties, wooden terraces that extend the interior space, and flexible closures that fully integrate the volume with its surroundings. The house, the kiosk and the jetties highlight the work in macana and teak, woods of high quality and resistance from the Caribbean region.

The project includes two two-storied modules located on the two cays that make up the small island, which are separated by a channel of water. A teak platform placed above the channel integrates the living room in the southern module with the dining room and the services in the northern module. The bedrooms are located on the upper floor, united by a bridge between both structures. The staircase continues to the roof where there is a terrace-lookout that provides spectacular views of the surrounding landscape.

the rock of Las Hadas island

Alberto Burckhardt

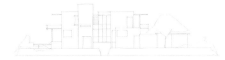

This project entailed the construction of a recreational residence as well as the recovery of a small island and its structures, which had deteriorated after years of abandonment.

Architect: **Alberto Burckhardt**

Location: **Rosario Islands, Colombia**

Surface: **12,900 square feet**

Date: **1999**

Photographer: **Silvia Patiño**

1. Entrance
2. Living room
   Dining room/Kitchen
3. Bedrooms
4. Guest house

This house is set on two small islands. The elements that define the islands are an integral part of the residence, including the stone barriers and the native vegetation. As a result of the environment, the house's design closely links the interior and the exterior.

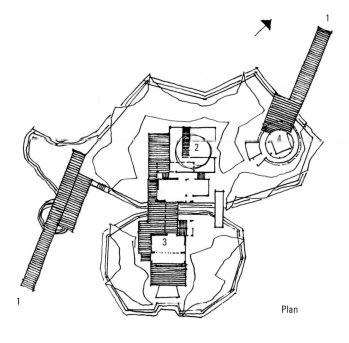

Plan

Two wood piers, the only way to access the house, stretch out on the northern and southern sides like outdoor extensions of the house. The arrangement towards the south creates a close-up view, in an attempt to capture an image of the sea, creating diverse visual relationships with a minimal gesture.

Despite the solidity of the structure and the exterior façades, the house has a permanent relationship with the exterior due to a succession of open but covered spaces, exterior terraces and a distant view of the horizon and the sea.

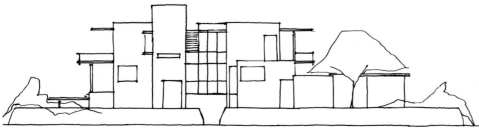

Elevation

An outstanding feature of the interior is the artisan work in macana, a wood typical of the Caribbean region which was used for the construction of the roof, the rails of the staircase and the details of the furnishings.

The guest house is composed of a circular volume, in the form of a kiosk, that is totally isolated from the main house. The module contains a living area, a bedroom and a bathroom.

The residences built at Capistrano Beach in recent years represent the typical condition of the beach front in southern California: increased crowding. Small, older homes are situated in the middle of narrow plots, while new houses aim to take full advantage of the land. Such is the case with this house, which makes the most of its surroundings and the available surface area. The interior features so much glass and light that the walls seem nonexistent and the materials seem to disappear. The architectural challenge was to maximize the space, the presence of the beach and the spectacular views of the landscape.

The architect's solution was to create a large, curved wall, which is used as a reference throughout the project. The wall establishes appropriate degrees of privacy and contrasts with the rigid and orthogonal geometry of the land. The public zone gradually becomes related —as the volume develops— to the exterior and to the beach. The different spaces that make up the residence's design are grouped along the curved wall, which contains openings and glass boxes that house each area. All of them have a distinct character based on their view of the sea or their relationship with the rest of the house. The transparency of the spaces emphasizes the views, links the spaces to one another, and highlights the presence of the curved wall throughout the house.

Architect: **Michael B. Lehrer**
Location: **Capistrano Beach, California, United States**
Surface: **4,731 square feet**
Date: **1997**
Photographer: **Michael Arden**

LigHt HouЈe

Lehrer Architects

Despite the site's minimal proportions, especially in terms of width, the architect created interesting areas and paths. The main entrance is located along a lateral patio, making it a deliberate, extended entrance that is protected by a portico. The volume suspended from the master bedroom has windows on four sides that blur the boundaries between the interior and the exterior. Ocean views and the presence of geometry in the project give this house a unique character.

Lighting was strategically placed to take advantage of the quality of natural light and to emphasize the architectural elements. The contrast of objects against the light generates special visual effects that change according to the time of day. As a result, this project of multiple spatial relationships continually offers new antidotes to discover.

An intricate, volumetric design makes the most of the lot's narrow proportions and creates transparencies and visual relationships between the different spaces and the exterior.

1. Entrance
2. Living room
3. Terrace
4. Dining room
5. Kitchen
6. Studio
7. Parking
8. Main room
9. Bathroom
10. Bedrooms

Ground floor

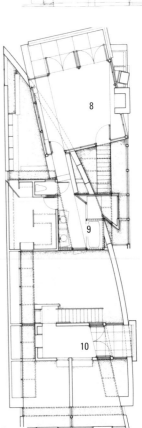

Attic section

The rigid and elongated form of the property breaks because of a geometry that creates diverse situations in the surroundings as well as different spatial relationships in the interior. The circulation and living areas have visual contact with the rest of the house.

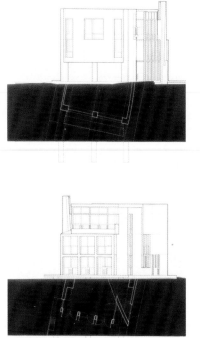

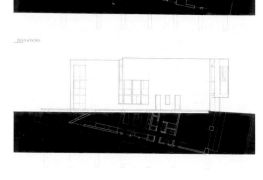

Elevations

The square frames of the exterior windows are repeated inside the residence as divisions of the different areas. The partitions frame each zone and create an interesting optical effect that makes the most of the beach views.

The site of this light construction, a typical weekend getaway in New Zealand, is a soft hill that ascends towards the coast until it reaches the beach. This inclination makes it difficult to see the ocean from the house, even though the beach is just a few yards away. Therefore, the grassland becomes a garden, defined by the construction and the hill.

The cabin's design had to meet the needs of two families who would share the space. The challenge was to create a flexible beach house that would solve the sleeping areas in an independent way. The architectural solution also had to provide a basic kitchen/dining room and a living area that could be expanded, if necessary. The plan started with two independent cabins, each with a loft, that provide a separate space and privacy for the two families when they are there together. If only one family is there, the parents and children can have their own quarters. The two cabins, located in the extremes of the construction, define the central space that is used as a living room and is linked to the exterior.

On the north side, a terrace —a wooden platform— stretches out and is lightly supported by the terrain, ultimately connecting the interior to the hill. On the southern side, where the entrance is located, there

is a balcony above ground level that is protected by a wooden pergola covered with canvas for the hottest afternoons. The inclined roof that covers the entire house reflects the sloping ground, the opening towards to the sea and the flexibility of the space.

The exposed structure, as well as the exterior and interior coverings, are made of wood, a material that creates a sense of lightness and maintains a dialogue with the vernacular constructions of the region. The zinc roof has been recovered inside with wooden panels for better thermal insulation. Sliding windows and latticework cross ventilate in order to maintain a comfortable temperature inside.

medlandſ beach houſe

Arquitectus

Two factors determined the design of this weekend cabin: the special needs of the occupants, two families, and the structure's proximity to the sea, even though the view is obstructed by a hill.

Architect: **Patrick Clifford Arquitectus**
Bowes Clifford Thomson
Collaborators: **Michael Thomson, Rod Sellas, Tim Mein, Giles Reid**
Location: **Medlands Beach, Gran Barrier Island, New Zealand**
Surface: **1,054 square feet**
Date: **1994**
Photographer: **Patrick Reynolds**

73

To resolve the slope on which the house is situated, the architect designed an elevated platform, reached by way of a staircase. The platform contains the communal areas of the house and the stairway connects it to the same level in the back part. The space below the platform is used to store water.

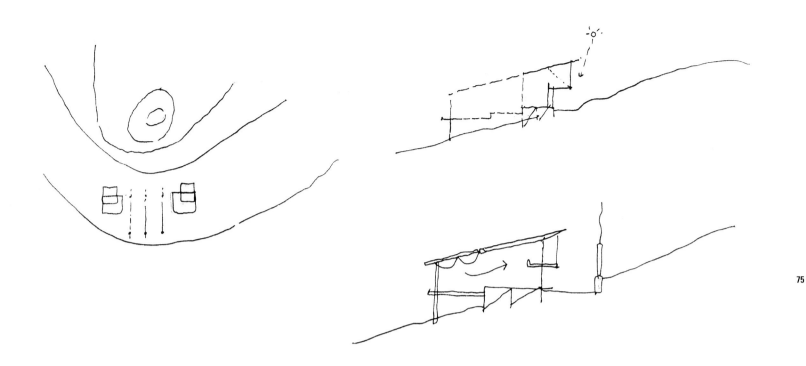

Wood is the predominant material in the cabin, in terms of structure and interior finishes, including the terrace and some of the furnishings. Wood emphasizes the light feel of the construction and its integration with the surrounding landscape.

1. Living room/Dining room
2. Kitchen
3. Terrace
4. Bedrooms

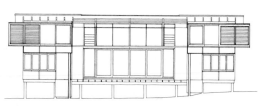

Frontal elevation

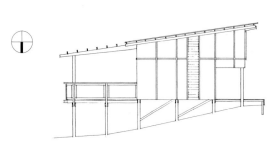

Lateral elevation

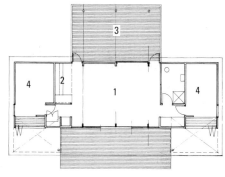

Plan

This summer house is located in a place known for the beauty of its rugged and natural landscape, on the southern part of Long Island in New York. While the setting includes magnificent beaches, it's also a zone of high density and urban development due to its proximity to big cities and its popularity as a recreational area. The topography is fragmented, like a series of folds, small dunes and shrub-like vegetation. The configuration of the landscape creates some nearby views, as if they were small gardens, in contrast to the open panorama of the ocean. The Berk Rauch project responds to this context by providing shelter and privacy from the immediate neighbors. The house also opens itself to the Atlantic on the southern part of the property.

The clients' needs inspired the architect to design a scheme of three different volumes, with equal hierarchy, that divide the activities: a wing for the parents, another for the children and a third with a living and family zone. In each module, the architect designed a unique, continual space with a close relationship to the exterior. The volumes' configuration in a rotary sense, like the drawing of a kite, creates an intense interaction between the blocks, yet permits them to have their own character and privacy. This scheme enhanced the relationship with the immediate environment by creating distinct visuals. The exterior space is shaped by terraces and by the volumes themselves.

In the interior, the structure and the exposed elements reflect the lightness of the construction. The columns and beams, in soft colors, reinforce the architect's intention to create a tranquil and fresh atmosphere. In contrast, the exterior part is covered with more solid materials to protect the house against the abrasive effects of the wind, salt and sand. The walls are covered with cedar planks, while the roof features panels of corrugated concrete.

berk rauch residence

Stelle Architects

This project manages with few gestures and an austere, formal language, to integrate harmoniously with the surrounding landscape and to create a tranquil interior space.

Architect: **Stelle Architects**

Collaborators: **Frederick Stelle, Walter Wilcoxen, Alexander Keller**

Location: **Sea View, Fire Island, United States**

Surface: **4,000 square feet**

Date : **2000**

Photographer: **Jeff Heatley**

The wooden pillars that support the house also serve as a leveling system that places the building lightly above the landscape of dunes and rugged vegetation. This design also prevents the accumulation of sand in times of strong winds.

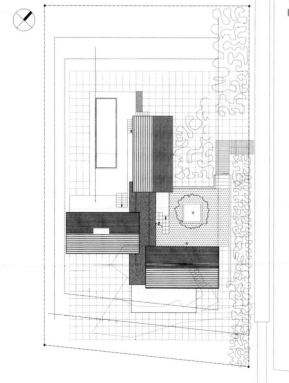

Location plan

The structural elements of the house are exposed and form part of the cozy, calm interior atmosphere along with the floors, window frames and dividing panels.

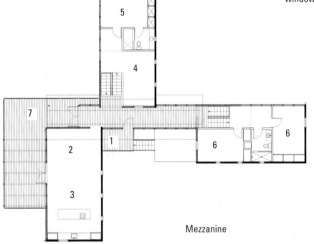

Mezzanine

Ground floor

1. Entrance
2. Dining room
3. Kitchen
4. Studio
5. Main room
6. Bedrooms
7. Terrace
8. Swimming pool

The service areas are treated with simplicity, emphasizing the house's relaxed and informal character. The kitchen, at the back of the living area, is integrated with the dining room. Both share a large table that has two levels.

This project started with an old house, of 214 square feet, that over time had become surrounded by much larger buildings with a greater presence in the landscape. In order to amplify the summer residence and make it appropriate for the needs of a larger family, the architect added on a 362-square-foot structure. The addition almost doubled the house's original size, yet the architect found inspiration for the project in the old house's light image and small scale.

The new structure, attached to the old one, provided more living and sleeping areas. The addition gave privacy to the different areas and maintained the ambience of a small house. The new building was designed to follow the same lines as the old, in terms of its layout, architecture and details. In an attempt to respect the original structure as much as possible, the architect built a transparent structure that serves as the entrance and as the nexus between the old part and the new. Its transparency contrasts with the solidity of the front façades in which only a few openings break the continuity of the plane, permitting a view of the sea across the entrance. The expansions between the different architectural elements reinforce the sensation of lightness. A series of piles in the front part and a wooden platform in the back raise the building off

the ground. A linear window runs along the façade and separates the roof from the principal volume.

The program of activities also repeats the original scheme, but in a more linear, diaphanous and continual way. The scheme is longitudinal. After entering the house, the visitor finds the sequence of the kitchen, living room, bathroom and bedroom. Towards the view of the beach, a continual and transparent façade crosses all the spaces, creating the sensation of a unique and continual space. The materials that the architect used agree with the environmental conditions. Most elements are typical of the coast and tolerant of the climate. The details of the principal elements feature painted cedar, stainless steel, the color mahogany, copper covered in lead and glass.

winer residence

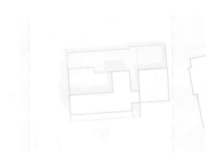

Stelle Architects

The project, a basic, longitudinal volume, is set into the landscape with great subtlety. The addition also respects the original character of the house to which it is attached.

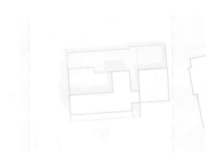

Architect: **Stelle Architects**

Collaborators: **Kate Evarts, Frederick Stelle, Conny Renner, Walter Enkerli, Verena Olson, Grayson Jordan, Jonathan Tyler, Alex Keller, Eleanor Donnelly**

Location: **Bridgehampton, United States**

Surface: **1,205 square feet**

Date: **2001**

Photographer: **Jeff Heatley**

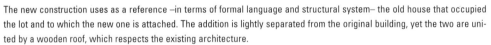

The new construction uses as a reference –in terms of formal language and structural system– the old house that occupied the lot and to which the new one is attached. The addition is lightly separated from the original building, yet the two are united by a wooden roof, which respects the existing architecture.

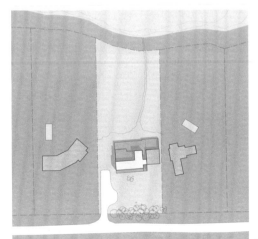

Location plan

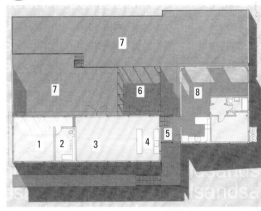

1. Bedroom
2. Bathroom
3. Living room/Dining room
4. Kitchen
5. Entrance
6. Corridor
7. Terrace
8. Original house

Plan

The continuous glass façade towards the northeast links the spaces of the new construction and relates them closely to the exterior terraces and gallery, which are like extensions of the interior. The view of the sea is the space's real boundary.

In the bathroom and in the kitchen, the furnishings and appliances are placed inside the space like loose objects, contributing to the continuity and cleanliness of the forms.

Barnegat Light is at the northern point of Long Beach Island. Aside from a fish market, there is little activity outside the summer months. The property, reached by way of a cul-de-sac, enjoys views of a large public park, Barnegat Bay and the Barnegat lighthouse. The building was designed for three generations of the same family and the idea was to share certain areas and to make others private and independent.

Due to the design's community-like characteristics, the lot was organized like a village. Each family was assigned a residence that can function autonomously. The interval spaces, including the kitchen, dining rooms and the main living room were designed as exterior areas. The development includes three independent yet adjacent structures that share common living areas. The first, the grandparent's house, has two levels. The first level contains the dining room, the kitchen and a porch and the second level accommodates the bedroom, dressing room, bathroom, studio and an open-air shower. The parents' volume has four levels. On the ground floor are the game room, a laundry room, a storage room and a work room. On the first and second floor are the bedrooms with bathrooms and studios. The fourth floor is a large, common terrace. Finally, a third, three-story structure houses a bathroom and a storage area on the ground floor and,

Houſe in barnegat LigHt

Brian Healy & Michael Ryan

for the grandchildren, bedrooms with bunk beds and a bathroom on the two upper floors. A large glass pavilion on the lower levels contains the principal living areas connected to exterior terraces, swimming pools and jetties for sailing and windsurfing.

The primary structure is made of wooden pillars, concrete beams and frames of wood covered with stucco or cedar panels. The ceilings are wood and fiberglass and the floors are slate and wood. A steel window frame supports a large piece of glass in the main living room.

This building is a development with three residences designed for three generations of the same family. On two, three and four levels, each house responds to the needs of its inhabitants and to the family in general.

Architect: **Brian Healy and Michael Ryan**

Collaborators: **Randee Spelkoman, Craig Scott, Allison Walker, Maiya Dos, Andrew Wilkinson, Michael Meggitt, Chris Jeffrey**

Location: **Barnegat Light, New Jersey, United States**

Surface: **5,376 square feet**

Date: **1996**

Photographer: **Paul Warchol**

Even though the project's aim is to divide the space for three different family groups, the architect maintained formal and volumetric unity, creating a single home. The different pieces that make up the project mix and generate diverse spatial qualities and relationships between each atmosphere.

East elevation

South elevation

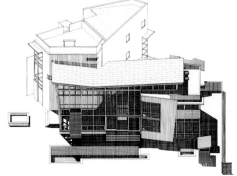

Axonometry view

Terrace

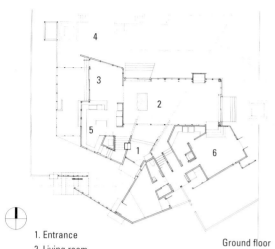

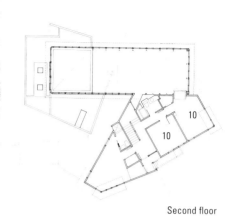

Ground floor

First floor

Second floor

1. Entrance
2. Living room
3. Dining room
4. Terrace
5. Kitchen
6. Living room
7. Bedroom
8. Terrace
9. Bedroom
10. Bedrooms

The Yallingup residence is located in one of the most well-known vacation spots in western Australia. The lot is sloped, which is typical of the landscape, affording the residents stunning views of the Indian Ocean. The project´s objective was twofold: to adapt the building to the irregularities of the land and to maintain a balanced vision of the overall construction. The home´s design –in a solid and linear architecture– is a departure from the typical wooden houses of the village.

The architect lightened the residence´s steel structure by installing a curved roof and wooden screens that softly elevate the volume on the side of the hill. The house´s rectangular form is unified by terraces with projections that break the curved roofline of the principal volume. The two floors of the residence feature glass windows and ample terraces that make the most of the stunning views.

The residence is structured on two levels. The ground floor includes the bedrooms and private rooms, while the second floor is a single space without divisions that contains the living room, the dining room and the study. The residents can fully enjoy the vistas from the second level. For the interiors, the architect used wood to give warmth to the solid, metallic structure. Sea air circulates throughout this residence of diaphanous spaces and white walls. The sensation of space continues on the terraces, where the interior and the exterior are related, creating an intermediate space between the house and the sea. Thanks to the construction´s elevated height, its residents can enjoy the coastal air currents that provide relief during the hot Australian summers.

This home is designed for relaxation and takes full advantage of its special location with views toward the north and west. The project also illustrates a certain degree of ecological sensitivity, since the house does not require heat or air-conditioning because it relies on the sun in the winter and on the breeze in the summer.

yallingup residence

Considine and Griffiths Architects Pty. Ltd.

This project links the residence to its surroundings in an architectural language that is quite different from the usual style of the region. The exterior areas of the house connect the architecture to the setting.

Architect: **Considine and Griffiths Architects Pty. Ltd.**

Collaborators: **Susan Griffiths Interiors, John Caro**

Location: **Australia east coast**

Surface: **4,300 square feet**

Date: **1999**

Photographer: **Jeffrey Considine**

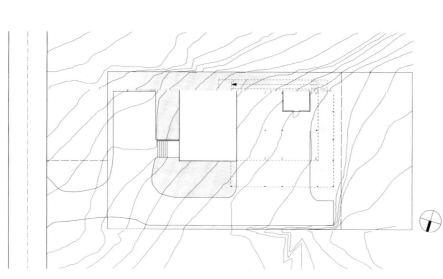

Location plan

Even though this house is located in a popular vacation spot and is surrounded by neighborhing constructions, it avoids urban language and presents a more light, rural architecture. This style is emphasized by the structure, which elevates the house above the shrub-like vegetation.

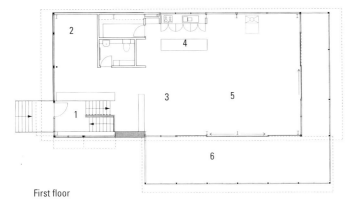

1. Entrance
2. Studio
3. Dining room
4. Kitchen
5. Living
6. Terrace
7. Playroom
8. Bedrooms

First floor

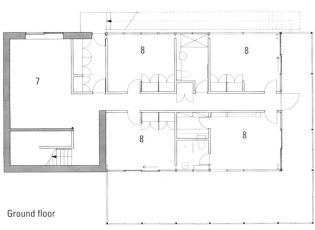

Ground floor

Low elements, like long benches and transparent banisters, create a continuity in the interior space. A view of the sea is visible from the entrance to the house and from any room inside.

Western elevation

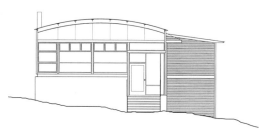

East elevation

South elevation

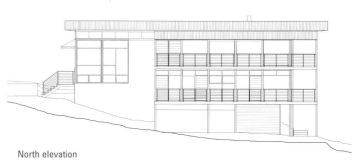

North elevation

101

This residence is located on Formentera, the smallest island of the Balearic archipelago, in Spain. The landscape features open views, horizontal lines and earth tones due to the wearing away of the land because of the strong climate, especially in winter. The land is rocky and precipitous and the vegetation is scarce due to the strong winds. On account of the geography, the building had to be placed on the high part of the plain that makes up most of the island. The house's location permitted spectacular views in all directions and turned the house into an object exposed to its surroundings.

The client specified and designed parts of the residence. A vacation home, the house had to accommodate a family and their guests. The concept was to organize the different functions of the residence to create flexible, independent spaces that could also be integrated.

The project began by respectfully introducing the building into the natural landscape. The architecture followed the island traditions. The house is a composition of volumes that repeats the model of bedroom with bath. The materials, finishes and height of the building make it a discreet object that merges with its setting. The horizontal mass replicates the lines of the faraway landscape. The only interruptions are large openings that frame the sea. The volumetric play allowed the architect to create

diverse situations in the interior that meet the requirements for comfortable living. Various terraces stretch out like extended spaces and can be used according to the season, the orientation, or the winds.

The island's traditional construction techniques inspired the materials, details and finishes. The bedroom walls feature an exaggerated inclination and are treated with a rough finish with a white cement base, natural pigments, earth from the local quarry and gray gravel. The other rooms are vertical and have a smooth finish. The bedrooms are treated like isolated elements that organized themselves across the living spaces. The owner designed and created the interior and exterior details and finishes.

Bill Wright + Nacho Alonso

A succession of volumes blend with the surrounding landscape thanks to the techniques, materials and colors used to create the effect of an architecture that emerges from the land.

Architects: **William D. Wright Torrance and Tomas I. Alonso Prieto**
Collaborators: **Miro Michalec**
Location: **Punta Prima, Formentera, Spain**
Surface: **4,054 square feet**
Date: **2000**
Photographer: **Pere Planells**

1. Living room
2. Dining room
3. Kitchen
4. Bedrooms
5. Terrace

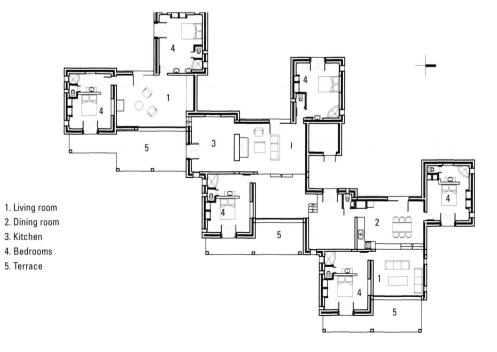

The volumetric arrangement of the house creates the effect that the interior and exterior spaces integrate with the landscape. The double openings of the spaces enable the side terraces to enjoy the immediate surroundings as well as the view framed by the house towards the west.

The kitchen is an open, flexible space situated in an area that serves as a hinge in the project. The small, star-shaped skylights in the ceiling complement the natural lighting and create a play of light on the floor.

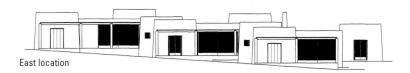

East location

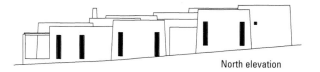

North elevation

The bedrooms are formed by a design that is repeated and articulated by the living spaces. Each bedroom has a private bath that forms part of the room.

Western elevation

South elevation

This vacation home, built for three siblings, is located in a rich environmental setting in Sarasota, in the south of Florida. With the Gulf of Mexico to the west and the Bay of Sarasota to the east, the Cohen House enjoys splendid views in every direction. The extreme climatic conditions greatly influenced the project's design. A natural habitat of tortoises and manatees, the region is continuously exposed to hurricanes, floods, strong rains and intense sun. The architecture responded to these conditions, as well as to the presence of the parents' house, designed in 1957 by Paul Rudolph.

The house is elevated 16 feet above ground level in order to protect it from floods and hurricanes. The elevation of the structure allowed the terrain to remain continuous, and the construction affected the land as little as possible. Protected by a forest of oak trees, palm trees and mangroves, the house is reached by way of an exterior stainless steel staircase. The stairway is the project's center that unites and separates the different activities. The pillars of the foundation go down 21 feet under the sand. Their presence is reflected at ground level with piles of reinforced concrete that sustain the principal body of the structure. The design also responds to the morphology of the vegetation. The habitable spaces are placed at the same height as the top of the trees, endowing the interior with richness and privacy.

Architects: **Toshiko Mori**
Collaborators: **Pedro Reis, Timothy Butler**
Location: **Casey Key, Sarasota, Florida, United States**
Surface: **2,796 square feet**
Date: **1999**
Photographer: **Paul Warchol**

coHen Houſe

Toshiko Mori Architect

The formal architectural repertoire and details, in a language with minimal lines, facilitate the integration of the building with its surroundings. The plane of the façade alternates between empty and full spaces that frame the different views. Built-in steel blinds filter the light and create a texture that breaks the surface of the large exterior planes. The window frames are made of steel and the combination of light, opaque and translucent glass responds to the various conditions, whether it be a glare or intense heat. The different types of glass bring variety and liveliness to a façade that otherwise would have looked like an airtight glass box.

The design of this house pays tribute to the legacy of the Sarasota School, a group of architects that practiced in the area between the '40s and the '60s. Characteristics of their work are reinterpreted in this narrow volume with minimal materials and details.

The house is elevated on slender concrete pillars that permit the continuity of the land and protect the residence from the possibility of floods which are so prevalent in this area of southern Florida.

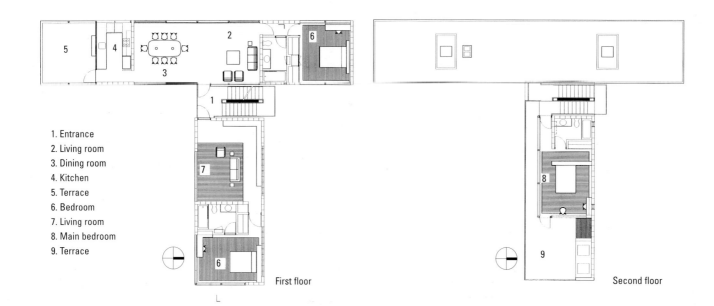

1. Entrance
2. Living room
3. Dining room
4. Kitchen
5. Terrace
6. Bedroom
7. Living room
8. Main bedroom
9. Terrace

First floor

Second floor

The garden features the same language and orthogonal lines as the house, like a mosaic of textures and vegetation. Little by little, the structure merges with the rugged natural landscape.

112

The project –especially the original house on the south of the lot that contains the principal bedrooms– makes reference to architectural example's from the mid-twentieth century. The result is an object that subtly takes advantage of the landscape while merging with the surrounding architecture.

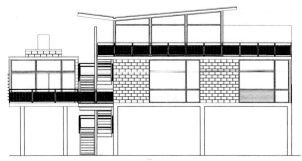

Elevation

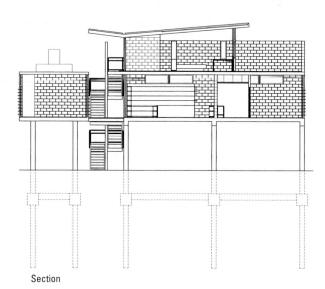

Section

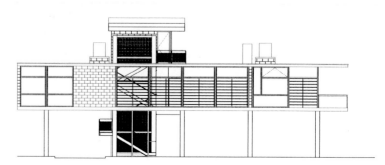

Elevations

The interior space is a relaxed, clean and austere atmosphere. The transparency of the windows and lattices of glass inundates each space with light and turns the crowns of the trees into the real boundaries of the interior space.

This project is located on the southern coast of Norway, an unsettled landscape due to the strong changes in climate over the course of the year. During the summer months, the setting is calm, with sunny days and mild temperatures. However, storms and strong winds prevail during the fall and winter seasons. Therefore, the principal challenge of the project was to respond to the climatic differences and to create a space that would serve as a getaway year-round.

So that the inhabitants could spend short periods of time next to the sea, the space had to meet the requirements of a small cabin with minimal residential functions. The formal language that the structure adopted makes reference to modern trends, as well as the local architectural tradition in terms of form and color. The cabin's limited exposure to the sea as well as its modest scale present a humble attitude towards the surroundings.

The structure was built entirely out of wood with different types of coverings, finishes and colors. A typical material of the region, wood and its different applications generate a varied, warm language with rich textures. The principal structure is painted a dark color for both aesthetic and functional reasons. On one hand, the color reflects the stones of the rugged landscape, and on the other, it absorbs a large quantity of heat during the day which it gives off at night, creating a natural heating system.

Houſe Lødner egge

div.A Arkitekter

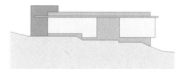

On the southwest side, a portico, also of wood, covers a longitudinal terrace that serves as the entrance to the residence and frames the path to the beach. In the interior, the spaces are distributed on two levels. The first contains the bedrooms, and the kitchen and living room are located on a level slightly below, which follows the natural slope of the land. The volume's simplicity is reflected inside the cabin with tranquil, uniform and light spaces that are related to the exterior with punctual openings that frame the views.

Though this small residence has forceful lines, it is austere, in terms of the both its minimal scale and its use of materials. The structure's simplicity made it possible to place the building in the landscape in a subtle way.

Architect: **div.A Arkitekter**
Location: **Eftang, Norway**
Surface: **860 square feet**
Date: **2000**
Photographer: **Inge Lødner**

The black color of the cabin makes its presence in the landscape more subtle while differentiating it as a unique object in the surroundings. Its longitudinal position, starting from the entrance area, creates an interior and exterior path that emphasizes the view of the sea.

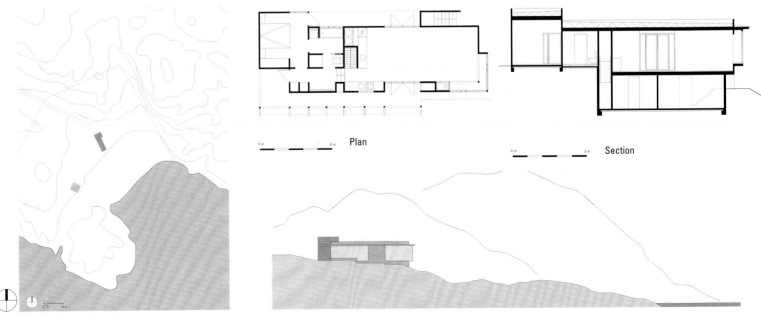

Plan

Section

Location plan

Elevation

The architect placed an exterior terrace towards the west to take advantage of the afternoon sun. Only a few steps from the main structure, the terrace is like a small rug placed on top of the rocky terrain.

Situated on the upper part of a hill and surrounded by a native forest of aromatic species, this house is hidden in the middle of a natural reserve. It also enjoys spectacular views of the sea in Palm Beach, Australia. Below the house, a rocky landscape reaches the ocean, while to the north, there are views of the sandy beaches and lighthouse of Barrenjoey Head. The construction is difficult to see from the coast because it blends into the landscape. The volume's warm wood façades look like a sandstorm, while the curved roof appears like a mirage.

The architect Philip Cox, who is also the owner of this weekend home, defined the project as an integration with the landscape. His design started with the building site, the surrounding landscape, the water, the sun and all the natural elements. According to Cox, the challenge was to take advantage of and create a dialogue with each element. The result is an interesting and informal experience as the model of a temporary residence. On one hand, the project reconciles comfort and privacy for a family, and on the other, it has the capacity for up to 100 guests, and contains a place to work. The architect considered this project an opportunity to demonstrate his philosophy and his ability to integrate a building harmoniously with its natural surroundings.

Architect: **Cox Richardson**
Location: **Palm Beach, Australia**
Surface: **4,516 square feet**
Photographer: **Patrick Bingham-Hall**

ocean House

Cox Richardson

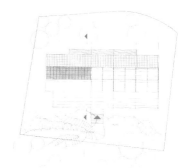

Due to the conditions of the site —especially the inclination of the terrain and the dense vegetation— the volume is planted vertically in three levels that "hang" from the upper part of the mountain. The entrance is created out of the roof, which is connected to the ground through a light extension in the form of a platform. The curved section of the roof creates a small atrium that visually dominates most of the house's living areas. The social zone occupies the intermediate level, and the bedrooms are situated in the lowest part of the composition.

The construction is partially supported by the face of a cliff. The building gives the impression of pulling away from the cliff, and the spaces are organized lineally in order to give each one an impressive view.

Though the house occupies a large construction area, it is terraced along the slope of the land, affecting the landscape as little as possible. The residence enjoys a view of the sea from the high part of the rocky outcrop.

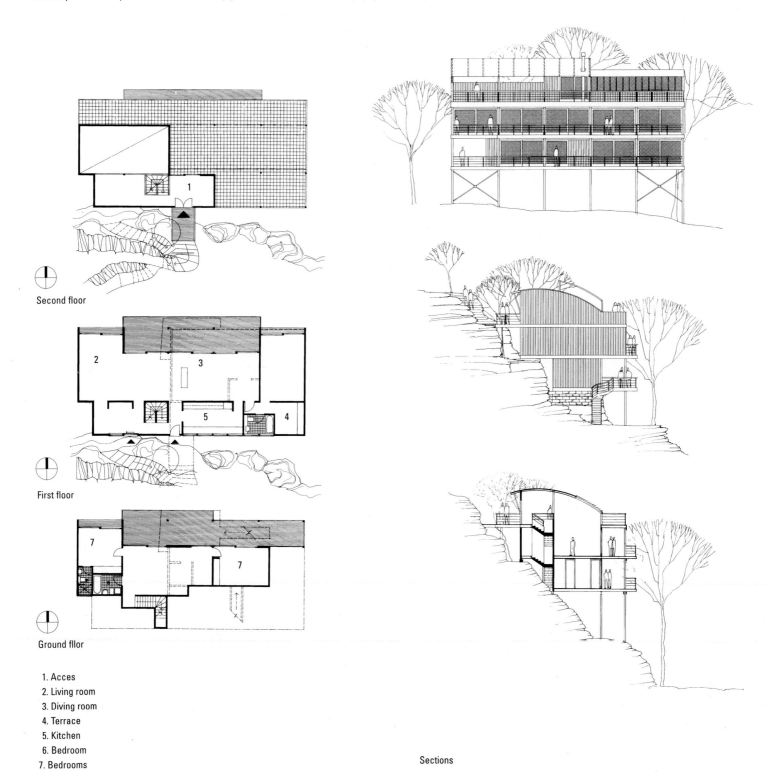

Second floor

First floor

Ground fllor

1. Acces
2. Living room
3. Diving room
4. Terrace
5. Kitchen
6. Bedroom
7. Bedrooms

Sections

The openings in the roof provide the interior with various sources of zenithal light. The openings, as well as the translucent canopy that covers part of the main terrace, bathe the house with natural light throughout the day and create a fresh and warm ambience in the interior.

This small summer house is located on the southern coast of Norway. The conditions of the landscape greatly influenced the project's design. The cabin is situated in the middle of a forest of oak trees, only a few yards from the beach. The architectural solution aimed to emphasize the boundary between these different natural spaces and to establish an element that reinforces their relationship.

The building is set into the landscape like a wall that divides –yet relates– the beach and the forest. Due to the house's configuration, the forest takes on the character of a private garden. A linear design is organized along a volume with narrow proportions. A double opening in the two façades, at the height of the dining room, connects the two natural environments. The volume's distribution follows the path of the sun: the bedrooms are located in the eastern part, while the living room and the terrace are located in the extreme west.

The project's formal language and materials accentuate its light character and consolidate its relationship with the immediate surroundings. A softly inclined plane of oiled oak panels covers the house and reinforces the sensation of lightness. The openings are presented as small volumetric pieces that intercept the plane, endowing the façade with an interesting mobility and enriching the interior space. The roof features exposed zinc laminates that emphasize the construction's light and economical character.

The interior atmosphere is tranquil and luminous thanks to the use of wood in lighter tones. The three steps that separate the zones of the dining room and kitchen differentiate the areas and solve the slight inclination of the terrain. The false ceiling continues the double inclination and wood of the roof. Light-colored tiles cover the floors, creating a durable, low-maintenance surface.

Architect: **Jarmund / Vigsnaes AS Architects MNAL**
Collaborators: **Einar Jarmund, Hakon Vigsnaes, Alessandra Losberg**
Location: **Norway south coast**
Surface: **1,290 square feet**
Date: **2000**
Photographer: **Nils Petter Dale**

ſummer cabin

Jarmund / Vigsnaes AS Architects MNAL

The design details, including light materials and simple elements like wooden panels, a zinc roof and sliding doors, establish a sober and elegant atmosphere.

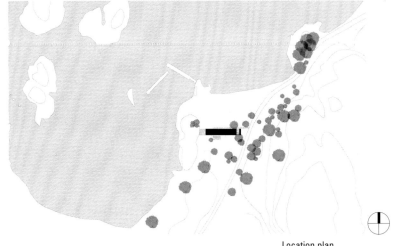

The elongated house is situated on the east-west axis in order to make the most of the sun, the distant views of the bay , the ocean towards the north. The entrance, a glass door finished in wood, breaks the continuous façade and frames the visual.

Location plan

The use of light-colored wood in the interior gives the space a certain freshness. The design and decorative elements, like the lamp in the dining room, the chimney and the kitchen cabinets, are specially designed to complement the architecture.

1. Entrance/dining room
2. Kitchen
3. Living room
4. Terrace
5. Bedrooms
6. Main room

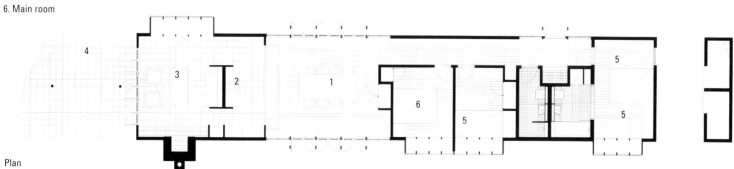

Plan

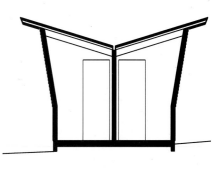

Sections

The materials used for the project, including zinc, wooden strips, and metallic veneer respond to the simplicity of the interior design. The openings to the exterior are like small volumes that intercept the inclined wooden plane, a gesture that gives the project a special plasticity.

This project used the conditions of the site as its point of reference: an 82x378-foot plot in an isolated area in the south of Baja California. The property has magnificent views on its narrow sides, of the sea towards the west and of the mountains towards the east. On its longer sides, the lot is limited by party walls with neighboring plots. The elevation of the land —on a plain 26 feet above the beach— creates a natural balcony above the Pacific Ocean. Located more than 12,5 miles away from the closest village, the land is part of a development. The only service available is water brought down from the mountains. A system of photovoltaic solar panels provides electricity.

A sequence of landscaped spaces welcome the visitor and make the transition between the arid desert and the house, located at the back of the plot. Though the sequence covers the entire property and features limited views of the sea, it is only revealed once inside the house, where openings frame and isolate scenes from the dramatic context.

The design incorporates construction elements, techniques and traditional materials from the region, which link the house with the vernacular architecture in a totally contemporary language. The composition is based on two main volumes that interrupt the lot's elongated dimensions and create a central space in the middle of both. This central area reinterprets the typology of the Mexican patio. The structures are finished with a fine mortar in a light yellow tone that blends with the color palette of the surrounding desert landscape. A series of walls recovered in local materials, such as Venetian- blue or bright red tiles, intersect and interact with the small buildings to create diverse visual relationships. The result is a series of open and partially closed exterior spaces reflect that the lifestyle in this climate. A third volume contains the master bedroom and is elevated above the rest of the house in order to provide the best views of the ocean and the mountains.

Architect: **Leddy Maytum Stacy Architects (before TLMS)**

Collaborators: **Marsha Maytum, Roberto Sheinberg, Michelle Huber**

Location: **Rancho Nuevo, Baja California South, Mexico**

Surface: **4,300 square feet**

Date: **2000**

Photographer: **Undine Pröhl**

cɑrмeɴ Houſe

133

Leddy Maytum Stacy Architects

This sunny getaway, envisioned by its original Alaska-based owners, was inspired by the conditions of the landscape and the isolation of the property.

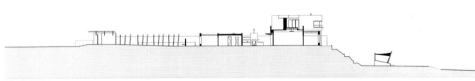

Longitudinal section

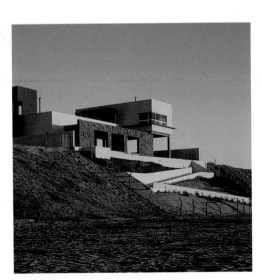

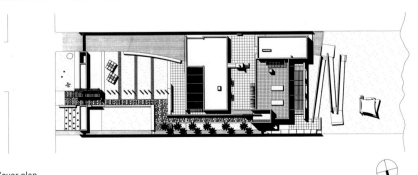

Cover plan

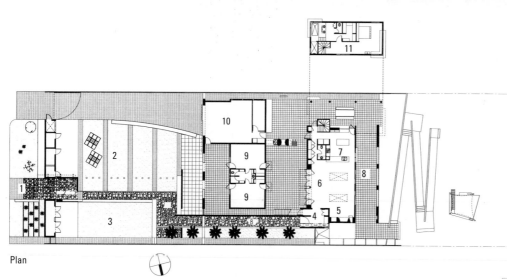

Plan

1. Entrance
2. Garden
3. Orchard
4. Hall
5. Living room
6. Dining room
7. Kitchen
8. Terrace
9. Bedrooms
10. Parking
11. Main room

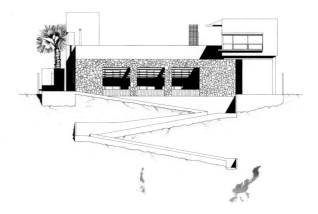

Elevation

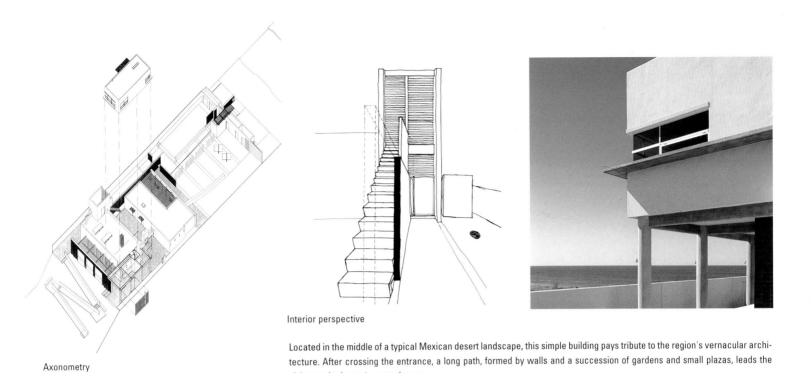

Axonometry

Interior perspective

Located in the middle of a typical Mexican desert landscape, this simple building pays tribute to the region's vernacular architecture. After crossing the entrance, a long path, formed by walls and a succession of gardens and small plazas, leads the visitor to the house's central space.

The structural elements, like the columns and beams, and the architectural gestures, like the stairways, walls and windows, form part of the project´s composition. Most of the furnishings are built into the architecture and express the same formal language.

This vacation home is located in Punta Piedras, Uruguay, a place that enjoys splendid panoramas of the Atlantic and that preserves the natural features of its morphology and vegetation. Dramatic changes in temperature are common, and intense winds constantly whip the coast. The elongated parcel determined the positioning of the house and the organization of the different interior spaces.

The residence is constructed entirely out of wood. Local artisans carefully placed each piece to fit with precision. At first glance, the house recalls a paradise of the southern seas. Vegetation conceals a large part of the ground floor, and the visitor first perceives two small cabins with straw ceilings painted blue. In reality, these cabins, which merge with the tones of the sky and sea, belong to the upper floor of this enormous house. The residence's large dimensions —including courtyards that help organize the circulation— seem lighter due to the use of local materials that reflect the typical architecture of the region.

The structure of the house reveals the family's needs. The client's requirements were crucial when it came to designing the project. The lot's proportions determined a succession of spaces that are open yet protected from the wind. The habitable rooms are dispersed in three different parts: one for guests, another for the children and a third for the parents.

After crossing the entrance, the first open space contains a heated pool that is linked to the guest rooms on one side and to the children's quarters on the other. On the ground floor, glass doors connect the children's living area to the exterior. The living room and the dining room are accompanied by a large kitchen that is connected to the exterior.

Architect: **Mario Connío**

Location: **Punta Piedras, Punta del Este, Uruguay**

Surface: **10,752 square feet**

Date: **1997**

Photographer: **Ricardo Labougle**

vally martelli house

Mario Connío

This large house recalls the regional architecture and makes the most of its location by creating interior and exterior spaces protected from the strong winds.

The house is organized around open spaces that are protected from the wind by different modules. Each module contains a different residential space and function, which in turn relate to the exterior terraces.

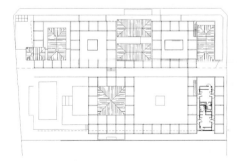

General plan

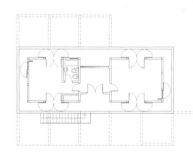

Module plan

The wood is painted white in the interior to create the sensation of luminosity and space without compromising the quality of the material. The structure of the roof is exposed, and its modulation and texture enrich the interior.

Elevation

The Bay of Fundy is one of the most spectacular –and turbulent– landscapes on the east coast of Canada. The bay is subjected to the highest tides in the world, and the difference between high and low tide is often as much as 53 feet. At the tip of the bay, high tide can reach up to 62 feet, the equivalent of a five-story building. Also the site of 82-foot waves, the coastline of the province of New Brunswick is the location of this family refuge. The landscape is a reef of granite stone, dotted with pine trees and scarcely populated –making it the ideal location for a private haven with an impressive view of the sea.

The project's design attempted to make the most of the surrounding conditions by placing the building only a few yards from the line of the high sea. From the interior, it's easy to forget that the building is a construction on the ground, or on the rock, to be precise. This sensation is reinforced by the large windows on all sides of the house, made possible by the lack of immediate neighbors. The building is also elevated to the level of the rocks which support it.

This home's design makes reference to the modern movement, minimalist architecture, and specifically to the Farnsworth House by Mies van der Rohe. The architect Julie Snow created a volume made of two equal bodies, one above the other. The volumes are aligned with the east-west axis and the upper one slides towards the west. In the extreme east of the composition, where the land slopes in a more pronounced manner, the architect created a daring projection on both levels. The structure is supported by slim wooden columns. The north façade –less favored by the light of the sun– features a stone element that gives the composition stability and contains a chimney and storage areas.

The interior is a tranquil, open and continuous space thanks to the distribution and the spatial relationship between the different zones. Upon entering the house from the north façade, an empty space relates the two levels. Continuous windows along the southern façade link the sleeping areas with the living area.

koeHLer refidence

Julie Snow Architects

149

This design of this house creates the sensation of being in front of the ocean, yet it avoids any literal references to a nautical motif.

Architect: **Julie Snow Architects**
Collaborators: **Campbell Comeau, John Johnson (engineers) Jack Snow (mechanic) Ed Young (builder)**
Location: **New Brunswick, Canada**
Surface: **1,505 square feet**
Date: **2000**
Photographer: **Brian Vanden Brink**

Bay of Fundy

Location plan

This house conforms to the terrain through a simple structure, composed of two rectangular elements . The pillars that form the structure extend from the lower part of the pieces and anchor the building to this rugged and rocky plot of land.

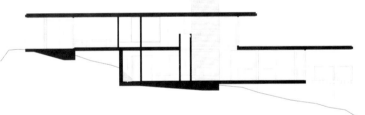

Longitudinal section

1. Entrance
2. Living room
3. Kichen
4. Dining room
5. Terrace
6. Bedrooms
7. Living room

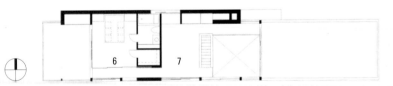

First floor

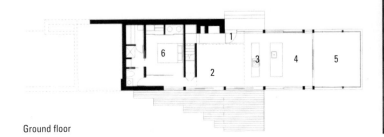

Ground floor

0   10'

The reference to nautical constructions is achieved through the reproduction of spaces and the relationship between the interior and the exterior instead of formal gestures, which would have made a caricature out of the house. The surroundings are more like a dominant and inaccessible landscape –like the ocean from a boat– rather than a utilitarian garden.

The clean lines and the prevalence of wood in the interior space generate a warm and tranquil atmosphere. The spaces are linked with each other and with the exterior view through mobile elements like sliding doors.

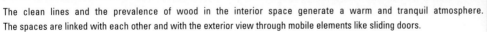

This house is constructed almost completely out of restored wood that was recycled from buildings constructed in the '40s. Wood, one of Australia's most outstanding materials, is used to build infrastructures and large-scale constructions like bridges and piers. Because of wood's resistant character, the architect used it for the project's entire structural system. However, the floor supports and the window frames came from the demolition of old warehouses. The floors and complete pieces, such as doors, were recycled from an old wool factory. Wood –the prime material of this architectural work– creates a strong visual image, with great formal and structural expressiveness.

The house's surroundings are typical of this part of the Australian east coast –a rough and hard environment. The closest reference to a building that fights against the elements is a port located under the highway. This road is an icon that symbolizes transportation and communication on Australia´s east coast.

The house is organized according to a simple scheme in the form of a "U" that wraps around a patio that captures the morning sunlight. A 41-foot long swimming pool is protected from the neighbors on the lot's northern side by a fence constructed out of wooden strips. Generally used for the construction of oyster boxes, the strips pay tribute to the local culture, since oyster cultivation is the main industry of Merimbula. The fence also protects the patio from the south-west winds that prevail in the area. A large wooden terrace runs along the entire length of the building, on the side that looks towards the sea and receives the afternoon sun.

The climate in this part of Australia encourages residents to spend more time outdoors than indoors. As a result of this lifestyle and to strengthen the house's relationship with its surroundings, each room has ocean views and its own exterior space. Three guest bedrooms on the main floor are organized like a suite. The upper floor contains the master bedroom, a small living room, a dressing room, a bathroom and a large terrace.

merimbula House

Clinton Murray Architects Pty. Ltd.

Wood plays the starring role in this house. Recycled wooden pieces with different origins make reference to various cultural elements of this Australian region.

Architect: Clinton Murray

Collaborators: Maxwell Murray (project director),

Andrew Murray (special finishes), Brian, Steven and

Trevor Jory (carpentry)

Location: Merimbula, Australia

Surface: 3,387 square feet

Date: 1997

Photographer: Janusz Molinski

The entrance façade is presented from the exterior as a low, austere and almost impenetrable plane. The residence is built entirely out of recycled wood whose different textures enrich the composition.

The different origin of the wood pieces created sections and discontinuous elements among the different details. The sum of these variables in the same architectural language is a homogenous and harmonic construction.

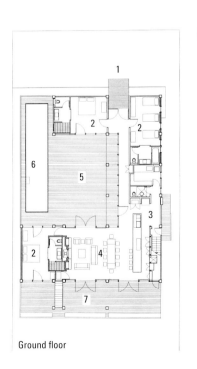

Ground floor

First plan

1. Entrance
2. Bedrooms
3. Kitchen
4. Living room/dining room
5. Courtyard
6. Swimming pool
7. Terraces
8. Main bedroom

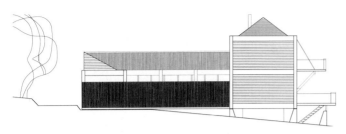

Western elevation

East elevation

The interior patio, the element that organizes and articulates all the spaces of the house, is an area of great sobriety and formal expressiveness. The openings towards this space are much more controlled than the large, continuous windows that open towards the exterior on the back façade.

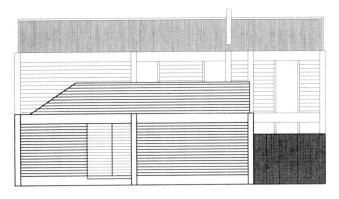

North elevation

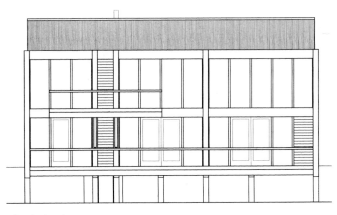

South elevation

Wood plays an important role in the interior. However, the floors are polished and varnished and the vertical partitions and the ceilings are plastered and painted white, creating a counterpoint to the materials on the exterior of the house.

This lot in New Zealand is stretched over the north-south axis and includes two zones with very different landscapes and views. The south part is occupied by a dense forest of lumber pines, which results in the sensation of being immersed in a large garden. The north side of the property enjoys more distant views across Mercury Bay towards the Great Barrier and Mercury Islands. The land is relatively flat and has narrow and elongated proportions.

Built as the summer residence for a family, the house's design was quite simple. The main requirements were dictated by the conditions of the site: to provide protection due to its seafront location and to make the most of the setting by promoting the relationship between the interior and the exterior.

The architectural strategy presented two buildings placed along the site. One is simple with square proportions and set amidst the forest; it contains a guest bedroom, a storage area and a play area. The principal volume is closer to the northern part of the lot. This building enjoys ocean views and contains the living spaces and the bedrooms. The concept behind this distribution of space is to create a combination of spaces that respond to the conditions of the sun and breeze and that provide protection from the possibility of strong winds.

coromandeL Houʃe

Fearon Hay Architects

Every room in the house feels the presence of the sea or the surrounding forest.

Thanks to this strategy, the interior spaces can transform from a closed space to a gallery that is completely open to the exterior. Large sliding glass doors can be folded to fully integrate the living room, the dining room and the kitchen with the landscape. The terraces on the east and west sides provide access to the beach and the pine forest. The building's alignment gives the upper floor, which contains the master bedroom, a special view of the bay and the islands.

The spaces of this residence and the project's objectives could best be defined by the word flexibility. The inhabitants of this summer home can enjoy various activities in close relationship with the surroundings.

Architect: **Fearon Hay Architects**

Collabortors: **Nil**

Location: **Coromandel Peninsula, New Zealand**

Surface: **2,688 square feet**

Date: **1999**

Photographer: **Patrick Reynolds**

1. Living room
2. Dining room
3. Kitchen
4. Bedrooms
5. Covered terrace
6. Terrace
7. Playroom

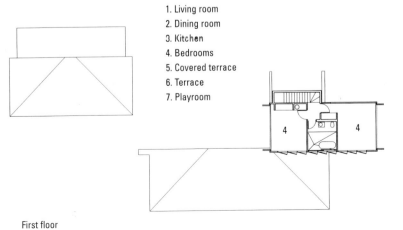

First floor

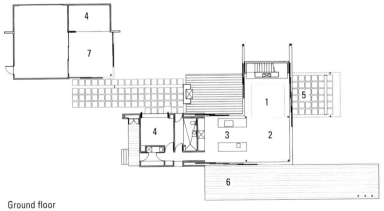

Ground floor

The house features a volumetric play between lively elements that contrast with other solid, heavy elements. The exterior chimney and the stairway are made of stone, while other elements in the house are made of wood, metal or glass.

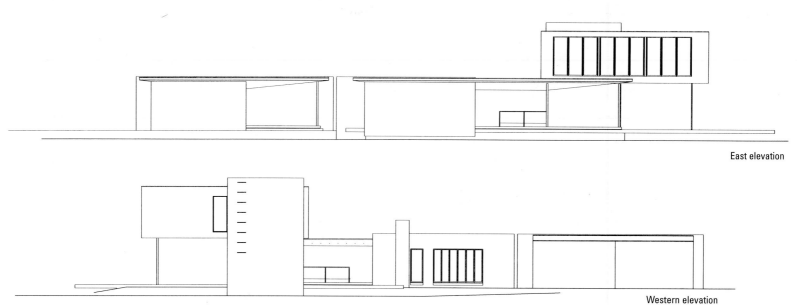

East elevation

Western elevation

The flexibility of the space is expressed by elements like the sliding doors, the folding windows or the curtains that can divide the spaces in different ways. Proximity to the exterior is ever-present in this project.

Long Beach Island is a narrow island in front of New Jersey's central coast that is used mainly as a summer resort. This house is set on the coast of the Atlantic Ocean along the island's northern edge. The property curves softly and offers vistas towards the north. The lot is located at the end of a narrow, dead-end street adjacent to a pedestrian walkway that crosses the dunes in the direction of the beach.

As is the case with most of the island, the street is as important as the beach in forming the perception and experience of the place. This house challenges the autonomy of the neighboring suburban residences by recognizing and reinforcing the common boundaries between the street and the maritime front. The building is set between the vertical wall of the street and the strong horizontal presence of the sea. The project depended on its relationship with the landscape. Other determining factors were the distribution of its parts and the use of color, which relates the building to its surroundings and whose hues will be lightly modified by the passage of time.

The building stretches out in a civic gesture to embrace the street. By doing so, it becomes a bench mark for public use that indicates the access to the beach. From the street, the house has a discreet

HouSe iN LoNg beacH iSLaNd

171

Brian Healy & Michael Ryan

presence, yet on the sea side it is opened and lifted towards the views along the coast.

A glass volume, placed directly above the sand, contains the primary social spaces and the master bedroom on the upper level. The guest rooms and secondary bedrooms are located in a separate wing. The principal living area is strategically located on an elevated level in order to take advantage of the views and the ocean breeze. A screen made of wooden strips protects the room from the morning sun. The floors and wooden furnishings create a sensation of warmth in large rooms that offer magnificent views of the landscape.

The wooden volumes were painted in distinct neutral colors that evoke the tones of the landscape. The large, double-height window in the living room is protected from the sun by a large screen of wooden strips.

Architects: **Brian Healy and Michael Ryan**
Collaborators: **Randee Spelkoman, Craig Scott, Maiya Dos, Andrew Wilkinson, Michael Meggitt, Chris Jeffrey**
Location: **Loveladies, New Jersey, United States**
Surface: **5,300 square feet**
Date: **1997**
Photographer: **Paul Warchol**

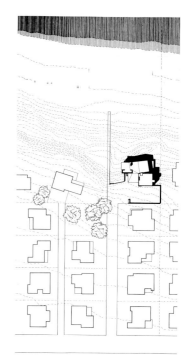

Location plan

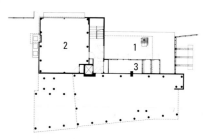

1. Entrance
2. Parking
3. Storage

Ground floor

1. Kitchen
2. Living room
3. Dining room
4. Terrace
5. Bedrooms

First floor

The architecture of the house is enriched by various elements: a composition of full and empty planes, various openings to the exterior (including small windows and large glass spaces) and a contrasting chromatic play between the different volumes.

East elevation

Western elevation

South elevation

View from the beach

The interior features a variety of spatial qualities thanks to the visual relationships between the different spaces, the tonality of the walls, the materials and the presence of light. The use of wood in the interior contributes warmth and unifies the atmosphere.

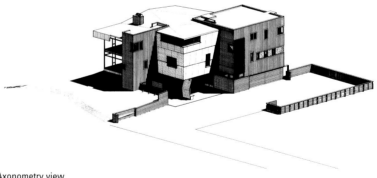

Axonometry view

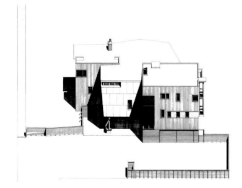

Axonometry view   Sections

Danielson House
BRYAN MACKAY-LYONS ARCHITECTURE URBAN DESIGN
2042 Maynard Street, Halifax, Nova Scotia, B3K 3T2 Canada
Tel: +1 902.429.1867 Fax: +1 902.429.6276
constance@bmlaud.ca
www.bmlaud.ca

Tagomago House
CARLOS FERRATER
Bertran 67, Bajos - Jardín 08023 Barcelona, Spain
Tel + Fax: +34 93 212 0466
ferrater@coac.net

House in Cavalli Beach
CHRIS HOWE / BOSSLEY+HOWE ARCHITECTS
32 Streatfield Road P.O.Box 622, Double Bay 1360, Sydney, NSW, Australia
Tel: +61 2 93281198 Fax: +61 2 93281189
chris@bossleyhowe.com

Reyna Residence
DEAN NOTA ARCHITECT AIA
2465 Myrtle Avenue. Hermosa Beach, California 90254, United States
Tel: +1 310 374 5535
dean@dnala.net

B House / M House
BARCLAY & CROUSSE ARCHITECTES
22, rue de la Folie Méricourt, 75011 Paris, France
Tel:+33 1 49 23 51 36 Fax:+33 1 40 21 69 14
archi@club-internet.fr

House in Bay of Islands
PETE BOSSLEY / BOSSLEY+HOWE ARCHITECTS
2/55 Mackelvie Street Box 47748 Ponsonby Auckland, New Zealand
Tel: +64 9 361 2201 Fax: +64 9 361 2202
pete@bossleyhowe.com

Casa Robayo
ALBERTO BURCKHARDT
Cra. 9 Nº 75-50 Apt. 502 Bogotá, Colombia
Tel: +57 1 321 7483 Fax: +57 1 341 7008
albertoburckhardt@hotmail.com

Light House
LEHRER ARCHITECTS
2227 Talmadge St. Los Angeles, CA 90027 United States
Tel:+1 323 664 4747 Fax:+1 323 664 3566
www.lehrerarchitects.com

Medlands Beach House
ARCHITECTUS BOWES CLIFFORD THOMSON
1 Centre Street POBox 90621 Auckland, New Zealand
Tel: +64 9 307 5970 Fax: +64 9 307 5972
email@architectus.co.nz

Winer Residence / Berk Rauch Residence
STELLE ARCHITECTS
PO Box 3002 48 Foster Ave. Bridgehampton, NY 11932, United States
Tel: +1 631 537 0019 Fax: +1 631 537 5116
ke@stelleco.com

House in Long Beach Island / Summer Compound
BRIAN HEALY + MICHAEL RYAN ARCHITECTS
51 Melcher Street, Boston, Massachusetts 02210, United States
Tel: +1 617 338 2717 Fax: +1 617 338 2775
brian@bhealy.com
www.brianhealyarchitects.com

Yallingup Residence
CONSIDINE AND GRIFFITHS ARCHITECTS PTY LTD
177 York Street, Subiaco, Western Australia 6008, Australia
Tel: +61 8 9381 1666 Fax: 61 8 9381 1566
cga@iinet.net.au

House in Formentera
BILL WRIGHT Y NACHO ALONSO
Apartado Nº 140, 07860 Sant Francesc Xavier, Formentera, Spain
Tel: +34 971 32 22 87 Fax: +34 971 32 28 09
billnach@interbook.net

Cohen House
TOSHIKO MORI ARCHITECT
145 Hudson Street 4th Floor, New York, NY 10013 United States
Tel: +1 212 274 8687 Fax: +1 212 274 9043
TmoriArch@aol.com

House Lødner Egge
div.A ARKITEKTER
Kristinelundveien 12 0268 Oslo, Norway
Tel: +47 23 28 41 00 Fax: +47 23 28 41 01
firmapost@diva.no

Ocean House
COX RICHARDSON
Level 2, 204 Clarence Street, Sydney 2000 Australia
Tel: +61 2 9267 9599 Fax: +61 2 9264 5844
sydney@cox.com.au
www.cox.com.au

Summer Cabin
JARMUND / VIGSNAES A.S. ARCHITECTS M.N.A.L.
Kristian Augusts Gate 11, 0164 Oslo, Norway
Tel: +47 22 99 43 43 Fax: +47 22 99 43 53
jva@jva.no

Carmen House
LEDDY MAYTUM STACY ARCHITECTS
444 Spear St. Suite 201, San Francisco, CA 94105, United States
Tel: +1 415 495 1700 Fax: +1 415 495 1717
www.lmsarch.com

Vally Martelli House
MARIO CONNÍO
C/ Ruiz de Alarcón 27 28014 Madrid, Spain
Tel: +34 696 516808

Koehler Residence
JULIE SNOW
2400 Rand Tower 527 Marquette Av. Minneapolis, Minnesota 55402 United States
chase@juliesnowarchitects.com

Merimbula House
CLINTON MURRAY ARCHITECTS PTY LTD
2 King Street. Merimbula NSW 2548 Australia
Tel: +61 2 649 51 964
motu@acr.net.au

Coromandel House
FEARON HAY ARCHITECTS LTD, FOSTERS BUILDINGS
30-36 Fanshawe Street, POBox 90-311, Auckland, New Zealand
Tel: +64 9 309 0128 Fax: +64 9 309 0827
fearonhay@clear.net.nz